Travelling with your Ashes

Heike Rentel-Thomas

Copyright © 2023 Heike Rentel-Thomas

All rights reserved.

DEDICATION

For Everton Thomas

When you took your last breath, when your pulse stopped, and I could no longer keep you warm, I was left with nothing apart from the promises I had made and memories of your skin. All beliefs and certainties disappeared. During seven weeks we tumbled towards an end that we expected but that was nevertheless somehow more theory than reality; everything seemed to be possible, and obstacles were simply there to be overcome. Love sustained Us and we lived, truly lived. Those seven weeks of pain, laughter, vulnerability and love, such much love, were the easy part of this path; a strange beginning.

And now I have to find a way to keep my promises, to show you the world, even if you can see it only through my eyes. You, my beautiful emperor, matter, and you will travel. And whatever will happen during this journey, I hope that I can follow you and find you eventually.

It took us so long to find each other, but in the end, we did and I am grateful for every second we had.

Please wait for me, wherever you are.

Travelling with your Ashes

Good stories need a beginning, a middle and an end. This one only has an end. In truth, two ends. The beginning is missing. Can there be a story, a journey without a beginning? Waking up from sleeplessness, holding on to nothing but a piece of cloth. Unable to move my feet, my legs, my arms or anything at all. The cat sitting at the foot of the bed, looks sad and hungry. I have forgotten how to feed him. Forgotten how to move, how to think. Forgotten anything apart from the pulse in your neck. Ash all over the duvet, feeling for the cigarettes, the lighter. For a flickering moment, I consider setting fire to the duvet, the pillows, the world. Remembering how to smoke. Cold, unbearably cold. Shaking. Yesterday's clothes. At least they must be yesterday's. Unimportant, immaterial. Your pulse, flattering at the side of your neck at 19:53. More ash on the duvet. The cat still staring at me. Green speckled eyes – yours are brown, but the cataracts made them blue, cloudy and bright at the same time. A sound from my throat, at least I think it is my throat, my sound. Feed the cat. One foot in front of the other. Big jumper. Grey big snuggly we called it. Over yesterday's dress. Cold. Feet on damp floors, basement flat floors, always damp. The kitchen, full of last night's events. Full of bottles, needles, jellies and pills. The sharps box on its side on the counter. The cat at my feet. Spilling his food over the rug. No matter. Kettle, fill the kettle with water. Muscle memory. Cup, coffee, water, milk. Pick up the sharps box. Yellow, rectangular with red writing, warning symbols.

Do not put your fingers into the box. Truthfully, I never have considered putting my fingers into the yellow box. What do I have to do with the box? The pills? The bottles and needles? I am sure I have to do something. Cannot remember if anyone told me. Yellow box, yellow folder. The folder we needed to receive treatment, detailing medicine, visits, observations and care. Yellow folder with your red form as the first page. The red form that you wanted to dismiss, in that one moment of fear, nearly a week ago. When you wanted more time, because you thought your last moment might be under the sterile, bright light that make everything visible and give no peace. There is no last page. There ought to be a last page, telling me about the end of the journey, explaining what has happened.

The fish screaming in his tank. Hungry. The fish and the cat, my cold feet, ash and the debris left. Sitting on the floor, next to the cat, in front of the dishwasher. Water from my leaky eyes. The kettle has boiled, and I am thankful for the warm fluid. Not enough determination to walk to the fridge for the milk. Pick up the paper lying next to the kettle. Receipt. One green T-Shirt, two rings and a silver chain. I cannot remember signing, but on the bottom, there is my signature. Clearly my writing. Swallowing more coffee, I wonder why there is only a T-Shirt. Surely there was more clothing. The green T-Shirt I have bought 3 weeks ago. 21 days ago. I remember your pulse at 19:52. The cat leaves. He will visit the neighbours for his second breakfast. Light begins to seep through the windows. I would prefer it to be dark. The darkness in cinemas and theatres concentrates the mind, allows us to see protagonists clearly. Allow us to immerse in stories, save stories that touch only the outside of us. But, now there is no story. Nothing left to tell. There is light creeping into the sky and the pictures fade. Time to leave the other world and return to the outside air. Feed the fish. Walk to the bedroom. Try to erase what is burned onto the back of my eyes. One foot in front of the other. Stumbling over the carpet. Some coffee spills onto the red fabric. I watch it settle. The air in the early sunshine is dark. Engulfing, all embracing dark that emanates from me.

Your skin, warm at 19:33. Flashing realisation, your ankles started to swell on Tuesday, wider than your legs. Suddenly, water, retained, unmoved, collected in your ankles and feet and I dismissed the thought. Had not paid attention or not wanted to see. But I did see, and remember it now, whilst the coffee sinks into the carpet and the stain grows fainter. Moving my body is unspeakably difficult. I have grown heavy. A new gravity, stopping me from just floating away and anchoring me to every spot I touch. Will they return your things? Receipts are for things that have been taken and might be returned. I brush some more ash from my lap. Stare at the tree at the end of our bed, the picture of autumn or winter. You saw things in the branches, livers and angels, a flute player at the fork where the tree and the branches separate. You blamed the medicine but enjoyed telling me about your visions. I tried hard to see what you saw but failed. Trying to find the shapes now, I stay on the floor between the bed and the picture. It is morning and I should take you to the station. Instead, I try to climb back under the covers, hoping for warmth and your breath.

I stare at the sheet. Dark green. Advice given and taken five days ago. A lifetime behind me. Dark colours make things look less dramatic, reduce trauma. All I can see is the flickering pulse in your neck, on the right-hand side, at 19:51. Time used to be important. Time measures important things, orders moments, events. Time recorded for incident reports, police records, lesson plans. Time to take you to the station, early in the morning, stopping on the bridge to watch the train grow smaller and smaller in the distance. How can things grow and become smaller at the same breath? Time, we had all the time in the world. Time structures our days, medication time, morphine time, blood pressure and protein shake time. I am the keeper of order, memories, the provider of small things, of dark sheets. And now, time has passed. That moment when you were warm, and I could hold your hand has gone.

I never had dark sheets before. I lie down on the space that is yours, breathe deeply. Faint, vague smell. More medication than you. I should probably change the bedding, probably, maybe, not now. Drawing the duvet around me, shaking shoulders feel cold, even with the big snuggly jumper and the duvet around them. The cold is rising from within me. Blood is warm, surely, it is impossible for a person to be cold on the inside. Reptiles need to bask in the sun to keep warm. You loved slowworm, legless reptiles, golden skin basking in the sun and burrow into the warm earth when frightened. I wish I could burrow into something more substantial than your pillow and what remains of your smell. My fingers claw your pillow. The dinosaur neck you wore for the past few weeks. V-shaped and lime green, it made you more comfortable. Your head so small that it appeared to disappear completely into the green fabric. Appearing and disappearing at the same time. Watching your body grow smaller and your eyes wider. Searing pain through my body. Knifes in my sides, in my belly, bile rising in my throat. Wet patches all over your pillow. Rain, there should be rain. But after last night's storm, it is calm outside of our castle by the sea. Underground, half underground, prone to flooding, but our safe space, our bubble. Nothing bad here – you always said – nothing bad here. I stare at the pictures behind my eyes. Your pulse, strong at 19:50. But you had stopped breathing. For a few seconds. With me staring, blankly and lost at your pulse.

And at 19:50 you took a deep, deep breath, swallowing all the air in the room in one big, greedy gulp. Paralysed, I did nothing but stare. With my fingers suspended on your arm, where I had oiled your skin. Aware only of the storm outside and your pulse. Your strong pulse. The life left in you, in me, in the room. I turn, my body a mass of pain, unbearable pain, scream, wail, I need somebody, something to hold me. Hold me so tight that all the little atoms cannot fly away from each other. Chaos, my chaotic body joining my chaotic brain in the grasp of a storm that cannot be stopped, calmed, tamed. Trembling fingers open the lid of the jar with the oil. Sara had made the oil, just for us, for our wedding, 101 days ago. I still cannot place all the herbs, all of the fragrances. But it has become our smell. Your smell. Your last smell. Opening the lid, you flood back, and I breathe you in. For a moment, I forget. Curl deeper into your pillow, hold your kaftan tightly against my face. Soft fabric, stripes glowing in the morning light. My stomach churning, retching, stumbling to the bathroom.

Beginning another journey. Not new, long forgotten path my body wants to take when my soul revolts, my mind disintegrates, the atoms circle out of control. I love you. All thought is still love. Retching, where there is nothing left. You have done that for weeks. Stumbling upright I catch a glance in the mirror. I finally understand why some people cover all mirrors. Mirrors reflect life. Ghosts have no reflection. Hidden, I should be hidden. Burrow into the earth, into the sea, into a secret place.

Unable to sit still, unable to control my hands, I pick up a bag. You always folded plastic bags, created a place for them. Always told me to find a permanent home for my keys. Laughed at my inability to follow this small piece of advice. Two bags, I really need more than one. Return to the bedroom. Next to your side, medication, bottles, tubes, tubs, the racing post, your favourite snacks, nuts and a cup with yesterday's water, holding the foam – headed sticks they gave us at the hospital. Shaking hands, unsteady fingers. Bags, fill the bags and stop. Stop at the cup with the sticks. Gently turning it between my fingers. Yesterday, in the morning, you could no longer swallow. You could no longer speak. Soaking the foam in the water and gently pressing it all over your lips. Chapped, dry, your lovely lips. I kissed them and prised them apart to offer liquid. Your eyes on me, on my face, my eyes. Asking for something, something bigger than me, bigger than us. Suddenly you were breakable, fragile, with swollen ankles and no words left for me to cling onto. Filling the bags, I notice the stains on the carpet. The footprints left by so many people, but not you. You left no prints on the carpet, just on my soul and a dent in the pillows and the dark sheets.

I find your hoover, our vacuum. You researched, evaluated and in the end ordered the smallest cleaner you could find. Five stars. It has been your machine, your first concession to having arrived. I clean, scrub, concentrate on removing their footprints, their breath, trying to preserve yours. Wanting desperately to keep only our smell, our prints, our presence. Yours more than mine.

Exhausted, I realise that it is a hopeless task. Indelible shadows of your past, engraved in the walls and the carpets. Sitting back on the bed, staring at the window. Outside is a world. I don't want there to be a world. It goes on as if nothing has happened. Nothing has changed for those outside or even the others in the building. Nothing has changed, but we do no longer exist. I close my eyes and see your pulse, as it was at 19:49. Screaming, I fall into the picture of your pulse. In my restless mind, pictures mingle, whirlpools of images. Clinging to the memory of your skin, without it I will drown. Holding onto the silence. I will turn my head and you will be there. Like you were, like you ought to be. As promised. 20 years. That was our promise. We knew that it was optimistic, but promised and swore that we would do 20 years. Made plans to fly kites on the beach, hold hands sticky with ice-cream and doughnuts.

I need your hand. Your fingers on mine. Turning my rings. Imprinted images, words. You had lost your first ring. Turned over every grain of earth where we had dug in potatoes. Sweat pouring over your face, drawn, wide eyed, until you found it. Needed a drink. Exhausted by the thought of the ring not being on your finger. You held me tight that afternoon. Never, never these rings should come away from either of us. From our hands, our skin, our souls. You had a dream, having rings made, just for us, with drops of our blood, welded to our skin. The eternal shape, unbreakable. Lost and found amongst dark clumps of soil. Rings, circles do not need beginnings and they do not end. Your engagement ring; Celtic, a worry ring. We chose it together. Mine simpler.

You wanted me to have something ornate. I wanted something old and simple. Both of us found what we wanted. You held my hand. In the shop. Dusty, selling mainly old coins. Just grinned, held my hand and slipped it on. Never, ever, you said, never ever will they come off. And then we walked in the rain. With a pledge in our hearts. Everything after that just formality. Not important. Mere paper. That was the moment. In the rain, with the blessing of the coin dealer, walking to the ice cream parlour. That was the moment. Future unfolding dreams no longer out of reach. Rain running down your beautiful face, glistening on the cobblestones. Our hands melted together, warm and safe. These rings, symbols, more important than those which came later. Our pledge, promise, 20 years to look forward to. Unbending, endless, eternal story of Us. Sealed by the rain and ice-cream in February. Your face, for the first time, turned young and soft and mischievous. Laughing at me and the ice-cream and being happy to sit on a cold bench with the soft rain dripping down onto your forehead. Being, just being, not knowing what was to come, blissfully stumbling towards this moment. My ring, on my hand. We could not decide if we wated to exchange the rings again, in front of the registrar and you giggled. Behind the mask, you giggled as you slipped the ring back on my finger. Whilst the dark thing was growing in you, unseen, unfelt, we were just happy.

Travelling with your Ashes

Should chapters have names? Words to tell me what is happening next? I have a difficult name. In the beginning, you did not want to say it. You did not know how. You practiced at work, at your desk, guessing. In the end you asked me and then practiced more. My difficult name, your unusual one. And even later, when you said it, when it had become part of you, you still managed to spell it in your own peculiar way. Did you know my name at 19:49? I am sure you did. But maybe you had forgotten my name and just knew my soul. You knew my hand, my skin, my voice. That much I know. I open my eyes; on the floor. Why am I sitting on the carpet, next to the bed, holding a bag full of small things? My phone bleeps from the other side of the bed. Too far away. Seagulls screaming, plaintive, protesting sound of the sea. The storm has ceased. Holding my head, I crawl back under the duvet. Shaking. Cold. Empty. Torn. I want you to fix me, hold me together. Tell me of the strength you thought I had.

I was strong yesterday, the day before, all my life. Now I am lost. Disintegrated, floating, trembling, unsure of anything. The phone is persistent, joined by the doorbell. Pulling the big snuggly tighter, I make my way to the door. Mick and Jen, both looking tired. I remember, Mick came last night. I remember him. Not letting him in, not talking to him, but I remember his presence. Solemn, he was serious and strangely respectful. I stare at him and Jen. Both holding me, hugs. Warm, sincere, no comfort. I need your arms.

Back in the kitchen, offering coffee tea. White, no sugar, both of them. The cat has returned, shouting his strangely demanding sad song into the room. My hands, flattering moths, are unable to hold the cups. My lips, unable to make sensible sounds. Curled into the corner of the sofa, I feel Jen holding me. Trying to soothe. Staring at Mick, sad eyes, watery blue. Not sure if he is speaking. Words have lost meaning. Trying to explain the strength of your pulse at 19.48 sounds churlish and feeble. Asking him why he came last night and when. Lost, lost and drifting in this room that is ours. Jen moves pizza boxes.

Mick had a call, from Kate, she was worried, did not want me to be on my own. Why do people not want me to be on my own? I am alone, you are not here. Other bodies, warm and alive make no difference. Loveless, what am I? Before you, I was me. Imperfect, prickly me. With a purpose, a dream. Opening my own school at last. Concentrating, focusing on my future, just mine. No children, no family, no ties, no promises. All gone, sailing on their own journeys that cannot include me. Pushing and crawling until I accepted that there was no-one. Arrangements, friends, lovers, work, art. I had me and my future. Not ours, not then. Not belonging to anyone, anywhere. Uneasy peace with my demons. They left me alone; I nurtured the carpet that covered them. My cottage, just enough for me, the fish and the cat. The cat hardly ever at home, nor was I. The fish not caring either way as long as there was water and occasional food. The summary of my life before, my past became my way to make things more bearable. Fighting against more pain, defending my skin against any intrusion.

Not happy, not unhappy, just me in the world I created.

Making things better, bearable. Not for me, but better for those who come after me. The children nobody wants, harsh and prickly like me. I can hold their hands for a small part of their journey. Knowing their shoes and their path better than they do, having walked in them forever. Hardly ever thinking of my own children. Gone, fleeing from me to a world of double garages and catholic eyes. Focused only on building a future, a school, a purpose. And then you came, we became Us and the world changed.

Mick speaks, penetrating the fog in my head. Words, in the air like bubbles, I can catch some, but not others. The phone bleeps. Messages, written words, heartfelt platitudes. Well meaning. The same question, over and over again. I don't know the answer. I don't know how I am. There are no words in me big or small enough to say how I am. Lost, wrapped in bubbles, only interrupted by the seagulls shrieking over the water, sailing on the wind as if attached to invisible strings. I need the water, need the beach, need you. Your hands, your eyes, your voice. Bile rises back into my throat. My feet are cold. The commode in the hall. I touch the arms, unused, not needed, too late. Tired. Mick and Jen leave so that I can sleep. They will be back later. Curling up into your pillow again. Closing my eyes.

And the picture returns, burned into the back of my retina. The picture, the moment, 19:54, when everything changed. When I became something that I do not yet know or understand. When you made me into a strange, scared, lost creature that can do nothing but scream and stare.

Uncomprehending. Disconnected. Shying away from outstretched arms as if they were covered in thorns. Chained to a dinosaur pillow. Aimlessly searching for clues or signs.

My eyes snap open. Sleep impossible. Deadly tired and yet – the etched nightmare too real. Your coat in the hall, over the back of the small chair. Above it the pictures we chose three weeks ago. Watercolours, local. The artist selling them to make room in his studio. We ordered them, pondered for a long time, which ones to buy. We both loved a clown on strings, but he was out of our reach. So, we settled on a green bottle of wine and two buoys. Excited when they arrived, you directed the hanging. You wanted to see them from our bed. In the hall, directly in your line of vision, they reminded you of the important things in your life. Wine, your Liberty family and Us, two floating bodies, inextricably linked by waves and thrown together by fate. Now riding together on the same current. A shared wave carrying them out further to sea. I take your jacket, my fingers digging deep into the silky material, your smell lingering. Your shoes under the chair. I have to move, shaking body, unable to sit, lay, stand even, but needing to move, to walk, to run. I am a runner, avoider, traveller. At this moment, in this bubble, where time and the universe have taken different paths, I need an airplane, a boat, a car. Anything that takes me away. But I have only my feet and they are unsteady. Still, I am somehow making my way up the stairs, into the light. Too bright, too harsh, too real.

The first time in weeks that I leave the house without a fixed program. No need to rush back, to do what is necessary to keep you strong. Just me, the seagulls and that sarcastic blue sky. When I had thought of this moment before, I had seen myself taking a deep breath. My chest hurts. No big breaths, no blinking into the new light as waking up from a nightmare. You not beside me to go to the station; not even back in the flat, waiting for me to return with treats and morphine. I don't have to do anything, be anywhere, nobody waiting for me. Just me and my twitching feet, ready to flee, to never come back.

When I left my country, I simply pushed the keys through the door and boarded a plane. I don't look back, ever. I just leave the pain behind. Start again, time after time. The beach on the other side of the road, an invitation to join the waves and escape. Become part of the wind, the never-ending whirl of past, present and future. No need for love, for anyone, for anything. Belonging nowhere and to nobody. Constantly travelling, running, no goals, no roots. No more words, no needs, neither my own nor others. When we first met, we talked about needs and desires. You had worked hard to not want, desire, dream even. You just took what was there. Wanting, really wanting something was a source of pain to you. You eradicated all pain, protected your core. And then, bit by bit, the crust broke, leaving pieces of shell all over the floor. The fragments of your armour became part of the new being, US. You wanted, suddenly wanted something, or maybe only admitted to it for the first time in your life. The struggle was hard, with many setbacks. Broken bones grow back harder and stronger, resist more. Your tears when you asked why you could not have what your wanted, needed, desired. Why you had to destroy everything before it could become part of you. You were scared of your ability to sabotage and hurt. When you grew backwards, into innocence and your own soul; when you started at out in this life, with the possibility of peace, of a place to rest and be safe. Suddenly I feel bitter. Me, standing on the stairs, ready to run, to forget, promised to keep you safe, warm and learning to be happy. I failed. Promised even a few days ago that nothing bad could happen to you, ever. Failed, not being strong enough, not keeping my promise.

The wind brushes across my face and I feel the wetness on my cheeks. No need to brush it away, it will only return. One foot in front of the other, I make my way to the car. When you were not working, had the chance to sleep long and leisurely, you declined to rest, came with me and waited in the car. Playing Pokémon on your phone, whilst I worked with those, who could not leave their house, their room, their safe space. Only later, when all of your demons were out in the open and we learned to face them, did I understand why you preferred to sit in the small space at strange roadsides. Temptations, untameable, uncontrollable, fell silent in the Us. Your protected yourself and Us by avoiding the times on your own, just waiting for thoughts to overwhelm, needing to be calmed and subdued. So, wherever I went, you came with me, waiting, with your beautiful soul struggling to contain the uncontrollable pain. And the Us, the new skin we created without ever really realising it, became your protector; stronger than all the layers you had created during your lifetime.

Stumbling through aisles, the light hurting my eyes, already stinging. I am glad of the mask, half my face covered. A burka would be a blessing. Floating through people, fruit, veg., dairy. Disconnected from the air, the sounds. Vacant, I find myself in the health food section. Picking up protein shakes, vitamins, snacks full of calories and promise. Shaking the pain of my face, holding the trolly as if it were your arm. Something in me remembers the cat food, staring at Jack Daniels, brandy, vodka and wine. There are special offers. Months of special offers, carried home like prizes, to help you stay comfortably numb. How many of these savings have carved lesions, left scars? How many scars have I caused by enabling you? Stare at the bottles. Amber, honeylike fluid. Self-medicating, protecting the clown, the emperor, the illusion. The moment, the picture, edged in my mind at 19:54, mingles and merges with the phantasy of smashing all of these bottles and watch the amber pond slowly growing until it covers the world. Drowning everything and everyone. Sounds muffled and dampened as if covered in snow.

I always loved snow. New, silent, clean world full of hope. Covering all yesterdays, hiding patches of oil and spilled life. Just before it snows, the air feels warmer, the sky heavier. I can smell snow hours before the clouds shed their feathery load. You laughed at my love for the cold, fragile structures of ice. But this is not snow, the world has muffled itself and does not know it. People walking behind glass, I am sure they are speaking, but the noise does not reach my ears. Is it me captured, imprisoned in a snowdome or is it the world? Not sure if I am looking in or out anymore. After fleeing from the flat, I am now fleeing from the shop, the light, the noise that I know to be there. Two familiar faces. Arms around my shoulders and all I can do is stare. The touch hurts. My skin has become too thin overnight. Friends, important, supportive, pity in their eyes, wondering why I am here, shopping. Staring at the strange creature I have become, urging me to rest, to be kind to myself.

I never wanted to go shopping with you. Hated the thought of Us being lost amongst mundanities. Tried to keep the ordinary, the chores to myself. Building a space for you be you, wonderful, contradictory, beautiful you. Nest of Russian dolls, each layer harder to shed, protecting the core, the boy. You, who never wanted anything, and took it all. Emperor, failure, clown, addict, beautiful soul. Your dreams, shared nightly, allowing me glimpses before you found words to guide me through the rabbit hole of the world you created. Your protectors. They had names, your demons. And I learned to see them, address them, walk with them, until you could see the crossroads and decided to take a path that led you away from the amber lakes. Decided that you no longer needed your medication. Won the fight against ants under your skin, sweat and invisible monsters. Too late, but we did not know that. Not then. Clinging onto the trolly until I reach the car. The air, real and cold, bathed in sun and dust brushes over my skin like sandpaper.

Fleeing back, stumbling on stairs, struggling with keys. In front of our door, some flowers, someone has sent flowers already. Why do people send flowers and cards with black rims? And next to them a parcel. I stare. Yesterday, I ordered some new, more suitable incontinence pads. Yesterday, I prepared for weeks of new skills to master, new needs, new ways of coping. Blindly, trustingly, I had ordered what would be needed. And it arrived today, the parcel. Yesterday, reality still existed. Today, now, at this moment, there is no reality worth preparing for. I touch the brown box, burn my skin on my own hope and leave it where it is. I cannot take it into the flat, cannot carry it. It will stay where it is until someone, anyone tells me what to do. We have no longer a need for dark sheets, pads, Jaffa cakes, blood sugar tests or morphine. We no longer need anything, are anything. The things that were of utmost importance less than 24 hours ago have become pointless and hurtful reminders of whatever could have been. I take the flowers. Lilies in a small basket. There is a card. Your Liberty family, true friends, colleagues, brothers and sisters in arms. Working hard, every hour they can, to keep the nation in wine. You left me with dozens of bottles. Months ago, I bought you a wine-rack, stored them flat and safe. You unpacked your treasures, tried to make me understand different qualities and aromas. I am not a drinker of wine, heathen in all things Baccus and you promised to teach me over the years we had ahead of us.

And seven weeks ago, you finally unpacked your glasses. Thin and wispy candyfloss glass. Delicate long stems, brittle legs of newly born deer. You had bought two, a long time ago. You did not have many things, nearly none. These fragile wine glasses, in their boxes, untouched, travelling with you, never to be unpacked, were your treasure. Defending you against sofas in front gardens and discarded lives. You said you would free them from their cardboard prisons if you ever found a home. At the end of your quest to arrive at a place that would be safe for the boy at your core. In the cottage, the remained in their packaging, next to your half-unpacked suitcase. And finally, in our cave, you unpacked one, held it into the light and filled it with wine for me. To teach me about the colours, the fruit, the sunshine captured in the deep red fluid. I am allergic to tannin but tried my best to follow the lesson. The bottles, now dusty; still lying flat, still unopened, unwanted, together with lottery tickets that have cost a small fortune and come with miniscule odds of winning are my inheritance.

Back into the twilight. The cat waits at the bottom of the stairs. He seems to be looking for something behind me. We both grapple with the emptiness, the new void. I leave the bags on the floor in the kitchen, creep back into the pillows. Staring at the tree at the foot of our bed, your dressing gown. Dark purple, glowing, regal. It used to belong to your mother. Your mother's legacy, her dressing gown and the cross from her grave. Not forgetting 13 children, some living, some dead. All marked by her pain. Genetics and nurture, or lack of the latter causing the wounds to exponentially grow. Like your cells in the end. Reaching a tipping point, there is no turnstile, no chant or recipe to halt the cascade. Once activated, hate and cells breed at an extraordinary speed. They poison, destroy and leave nothing but bitterness behind.

The covers feel clammy and stiff, and after the sunlight outside, the walls are darker than I remember. I sleep for a while, wake up when the doorbell rings. Dreamt of your face, not a dream, surely, you will be there, smiling from your Dinosaur pillow and ask for your morphine. Mick with his solemn expression, trying to hold me, words stroking my hair, spilling all over the grey snuggly jumper.

Confused, I retreat into the corner of the sofa. Safe. Small. Pity magnifies pain into unbearable agony. Mick, who has been your friend from your first meeting. Mick, my brother in spirit, who used to cook pork during the night; in the big house, years ago, before I lost me. Before my dreams of family ended and my children left. Mick was there during the dark times, when I made cake that nobody would eat, just to forget the pain. When I frantically scrubbed walls and floors to erase my dreams. Mick was your brother in so many ways. You had taken some of the same roads. But he took a different turn when he still had time. You had not known each other long, when both of you recognised something in each other that was familiar and bonded you without words. He does not cry, not now, not here. But I know he is swallowing hard. I can see his neck working, preventing his own pain to mingle with mine. Tearing, searing pain, his and mine, different and yet the same. If I close my eyes and open them quickly, you might just sit there, next to him. Scheming, mischievous, asking him over and over again to look after me. He is trying. He is doing his best, but lost as we are, we just sit here, staring at the sky outside. I remember him, bowing his head, with his hands folded, strangely respectful when they took you away. Why do we pay respect to our dead, if they earned or not? Why bow in front of a body, a coffin? They took you away. I somehow remember the outline of a trolley, upright, easier for the stairs I presume. A trolley like those you used to move cartons of wine. And Mick gently pushing me back into the living room so that I would not witness this final exit.

Maybe, if I had not told you to go, at 19:54, during the storm, you might still be here. Not flown, not left me, Us, the cat. Maybe if I had insisted that you look after yourself, earlier, when we had time, nothing of this might have happened. Doubling over in my corner, forcing the screams back into my throat. No room for words, for gestures. I need to see you, one more time, walking away from me, catching a train, knowing that you will be home later. The universe is claiming back what I had saved on special offers. And there is interest. Payback for enabling you.

Playing with your demons as if they were pets. Overestimating my strength, as I often do. Not judging, not trying to change. Clichés are sometimes more apt than reality. I never tried to change you, your habits, your self-destruct button, your dark moods and disregard for yourself. You never tried to change me, my prickles, my eccentrics shoes and the chaos of my soul; our scars became part of us. Two solitary bees sharing the same petal. Two lone wolves building a cave for the winter. Accepting, exploring, healing each other's wounds. And just as we both grew well, grew skin that could protect both of us, you grew new cells - inside you, pushing the healthy ones out of the way. Claiming what we had built, taking what was Us. You could fly away, knowing that I would be there to close your eyes, hold your hand, share that last breath. Who will close my eyes? I had trusted that it would be you. Doubling up again, in the corner of the sofa, with Mick's watery eyes on this body that has lost the heart to speak, I swallow the screams until they form a boulder at the top of my throat.

Yesterday I was strong. Purpose, you, us, looking after your body whilst holding your soul. My arms supporting your weight, my hands oiling your skin, tending to bedsores and schedules. Calling for help, nurses with calm voices and medication in vials. Holding your shoulders to steady the retching. Watching you and protecting your sleep. Now, small, shrinking in the corner of the sofa. Nothing to say and yet choking, imploding. Restless and tired, reaching into nothing and nowhere. My phone demanding attention. The doctor. Paperwork. I did not expect paperwork, questions. What did I expect? What do I know about the formalities of your leaving? He is hurried, just as he had been when he came to see us. He came that day to sign the red form. A choice, yours, mine, ours. For them not to break your bones, turning machines into your guardians, not to try to preserve what destined to be lost. He came, in the early evening, after his allocated hours. Complaining about life being busy, too busy to handle. Dropped in on his way home, making it easy for him. One signature and it was all done. They would not poke and prod, connect and administer. You knew what it meant, you made a choice, rational, unflinching, detached. And that you later, for one brief moment, regretted your choice, tried to undo it, did not invalidate this moment. The only time, you were frightened, panicked, ready to give, risk anything for a few more moments; under bright hospital lights, devoid of shadows, cruelly exposing your ribs and your cheekbones under those unnaturally large eyes.

We held hands whilst you signed, warm, sure that whatever we did was right. The form, neatly nestling in the yellow folder that was needed to organise our journey, providing space for nurses to sign for their visits and drugs, was in the end on needed, and I am glad.

Now, in my corner on the sofa, his voice again. Still brisk, still hurried, still devoid of warmth. More paperwork, this time not for you to sign. Your hands will never again hold a pen. The lovely fountain pen I bought to replace one you had lost many years ago and you still remembered with fondness and regret, you will never hold it again. The doctor's voice continues to ask questions and asks to confirm what he already knows. Clinical information, recorded last night and retold over the phone. I have a form attesting an expected death. He will do the rest from here. I have no idea what the rest is, but it does not matter much anyway. Mick brings me coffee. I choke. Staring at the wall of books, I am trying to understand the call. Trying to look for something warm in the doctor's voice. It would not matter, if it had been there, but absence feels strangely hurtful. He has no reason to care, and I have no right to expect him to. And yet, something hollow is left. Wanting to run, explode, disappear, shout, become invisible, all I can do is draw my feet closer to myself. One of your daughters calls. Offers help with sorting through your things. Why would I sort through your things? I know where they are. They are tidy, ironed, in their rightful place. In the world we built for us, part of it. She tells me that she knows how I am feeling. How can she know, if I have no idea? How does she find words, practical, logical, designed to calm, to take control over my uncontrollable pain? Stronger than me, in this moment, much stronger.

When we moved into our cave, you unpacked the books. You ordered them by size, and I have not found the time to organise them in any other way. If I concentrate on the books in the shelves, maybe, I can take in her words. She wants to take control, organise, own. Nothing of this can be owned, controlled. Cascading thoughts, waterfalls and rapids that cannot be negotiated. A path, slippery and changing cannot be tamed. Swimming under water, breathless in black, inky fluid. I remember them crying all over you, over your chest, your face. All of them crying, drowning you in their sadness. There was no need then. I remember staring at them, their tears. Telling me just how bad things were, when, really, they were easy. No need to be sad. Not then. No need to be practical now. Out of sink, either them or me. I am not sure who. So, I say little. Nod, pointless as she cannot see it.

My hands draw deeper into the sleeves, nails, scratching my wrists. Something other to feel. Your youngest. Hysterical, high pitched. Her voice piercing the air, reaching Mick and Jen, cutting through me. She has made a terrible error, she says. This child you loved most, hurt most, feared most. 'Keep your enemies close', you had said, pointing at her. You might have known what was to come, you might, in your morphine hazed dream, hoped that things changed. But nevertheless, you asked her to look after me. Of all of them, you asked the most fragile, most combustible child to look after a touchy, injured bird. Her voice drags me back. Consonants fly like daggers. I have little recollection of the time after 19:53. All I can see is your face, one eye half open, aimlessly looking at me. When your soul flies, clinging onto another one's wings, it is impossible to remain where the others are. I did not even try.

I called them, I had promised to call and your youngest took charge. She needed to, always needs to take charge. And I let her. At least I think I did. Uncouth, large, shimmering, dazzling child of yours. She wears your eyes and your humour. Her vulnerability and fragile spirit are yours and for all of that I love her. Her name on the paperwork, I had no idea, maybe she did not understand the consequences either. Responsible for cost, decisions, for what is left of Us. For your beautiful body, stiff and broken, alone somewhere. The body I can no longer keep warm. I have failed you. Did not keep you safe. Did not keep you alive, did not keep my promise. Severed promises, broken body at 19:54. And now she needs money. A lot. She had made a mistake. She had not thought it would be so expensive. Had not calculated coffin, paperwork and flowers. You and I, we had talked about the After. Theory, preparing for the inevitable. Still somewhere in the depths of our hearts tried to believe that it would not come. This moment. This unbearably moment in the corner of the sofa.

We had made plans. But you had not written them down. Neither of us had thought of using a pen to capture your wishes. It did not seem to be necessary. Necessary was to keep us warm and the pain at bay. You had nothing to leave to anyone, and you had whispered what you wanted with what little there was into my ears over the weeks that we had to prepare. That was enough. Only four days before the 25th of March had we tried to organise things. A friend, or at least someone we thought of as a friend, had come. With pen and paper. She wrote your words. But you did not get further than the guestlist. With me at the top. Your queen, broken, black crow, at the top of a list that was far too long. There are still restrictions on mourners. One of your daughters, the one who worries too much, at a time when you were still very much the Don, was frightened that she and her brother might not be welcome. Not blood. We talked, you had six children, you said. Not all blood, but all yours. No-one not welcome, you said. You did not care about blood, about names. You did not even care about the bad blood you had unwittingly, unwillingly sown.

You loved them all equally, not enough, but with all your strength. You had laughed at their squabbles, not, until the end, taking your part of the responsibility, which had weighed so heavy on you. Unacknowledged guilt weighs heavier. Your youngest's voice brings me back into the room with   a   jolt. Flowers, she says, your name in flowers. Pressed into hard, unyielding shapes. 50 Pounds a letter. Your name is long. Orders of service. Photographs and a preacher. A hearse and a limousine for the family. More than expected. My lips, dry, chapped, open and move. This is not what we had planned. This is not who you are. Wherever you are now, please tell her. Pauper's funeral she says, not for her father. The bolder in my throat grows. Unable to speak, unable to defend us, defend you. Letting you down yet again. I need to cash in your pension, she said. Pension? I had not thought of it. We had not thought of formalities involving doctors and funeral directors. You have left me 16 hours ago. I can still feel your cold skin, see your pulse at 19:53. They know a funeral place in Croydon, she says, who offers a payment plan. I once had a payment plan for double glazing and a sofa. I try to say no. Never been very good at it, worse now.

Weak, I am weak, no fight left. The alley cat of my youth buried under the rubble of years. Flew last night with you. On the waves of the storm, your soul and my strength. They will take you back. Back to the place you left, of your own free will, vowing never to return. Left for the sea, for Us, for freedom, to become You, to become Us. But they will take you back. Own you, take charge, organise; claim what cannot be owned. Vengeful, hurt love will take you back to the place with sofas in front gardens, shrill voices and hoop earrings.

Mick makes some calls, looking for ways to find money. Maybe your company? You had once dreamt of everything being taken care of. But then, you always had dreams and believed them to be real. Jen holds my shoulders in place. My shoulders that should not be bone and flesh, they should be wings to take me to you. I feel your skin, as it grew colder and harder. I know that your body, now in a cold place for storage, is not your soul. And yet, I want you to be warm, breathing and not alone. Not labelled, waiting to return to the place of your youth. They labelled my children when they were born. Little armbands with their names and a chain of numbers. Logged, documented, declared living. Now someone has attached your name and a number to you, logged, documented, declared dead. More respect for the dead, at least on the surface. But how can I know that they care for you, in this cold box, that they are kind and gentle and preserve the essence of you? Newborns and their mothers are connected by those little armbands. There will be no confusion, there are returned to each other. Why did nobody give me a copy of your label? How can they find me when you call? Stupid thoughts, of course you cannot and will not call for me. Your pulse has stopped, your blood clotted in your veins, your voice silent for the rest of time. And I cannot wrap you up, keep you warm and safe. You are gone, flew away and what was left, they have taken away to do what people have, pay respect to a body that has become useless, surplus, no longer needed by the soul that once inhabited your beautiful body.

Shrinking further and further into my corner, I try to concentrate on the things I seem to have to do. It appears that I must find money, that I have to accept, get better and not be on my own. I have to answer questions and wash my face. I must feed the cat and the fish, and some day take care of your things. Apparently, time will make things better.

Come home. Call me. Anything. Give me a sign. What do you want me to do? What is the right thing? Help me to make things right. Help me to make them understand. You cannot be pressed into letters of flowers, orders of service, and you would spit at the preacher. And yet, there is nothing to stop it. Your wishes overruled by payment plans. No power strong enough to change their minds and your daughter's signature. Our voices silenced in the end. Immaterial wishes, insignificant love. Edited out with a fine pen, stroke by stroke over the past seven weeks. Why did we not notice? Notice the subtle and slow change, the intentions to take, to hold, to claim. We should not have trusted that those who tormented you when you were well had somehow become your supporters. As you had grown tired and unable to fight, you made clear that I was your voice, spoke for your soul. But now, with everything done, taken, claimed, I must grow smaller, until nobody can see me and my pain that has grown larger than me, swallows me and takes me to you.

Unsure, unsteady, I set one foot in front of the other. Senseless, pointless, unlovable, prickly me. Pushing people away, hiding, looking for you and your smell. Looking for the bottles that held your life, and in the end took it. Comfortably numb. Until you wanted to feel, wanted to live. Until we were beyond having time. Days, weeks must pass by, I am sure the world outside of Us has not stopped. I am observing myself. The permanent sickness has become my steady companion again. As it was many years ago, before the long journeys, when many cuts were still young and fresh, and many were still to come.

A lifetime before you. My throat closing. Unable to swallow. Food is life, so they say. With you, I could eat. We never talked much about my years of hunger. Not hungry, just jaws unable to accept life. My demons. The stories my mother had to tell me to make me eat. Four years old, and the inability to swallow, to chew; the terror steaming on plates in front of me. Distracted, I might open my mouth. Later, the lunch left on a warming plate, flushed away, wiping the rim clean. My mother never asked what happened to make my lips welded together. She never wanted to know why this small being did not want to take life of a plate. In the end there came a white hospital bed, feeding regime, missing my son for long 12 weeks, still alive, still screaming inside, with my lips still closed. Lucky to be alive, so they said, not understanding, not seeing what was with in front of them for so long.

My demons, like yours can play like pets, sleep for years. Hibernate, rest, until the fear returns. A noise, a smell, a movement and they are all back. Keeping them under control takes strength. None left now. They feed of pain, living in wounds like maggots. Your feet at night, searching for mine, kept me safe. On Sundays, we walked to the shop. The shopkeeper, who knew what you drank and always had my cigarettes ready. Seven weeks ago, he began to ask after you. He was worried and prayed for you, for Us. On those Sundays, those before the doctor's verdict, you had your bottle of amber and I the biggest tub of ice-cream. Chocolate, amber in hand, we walked back. Your fingers intertwined with mine. Your eyes, unused to the wind brushing in from the sea, watering. Creeping deeper into your jacket, useful for city life, too thin for our Sunday walk, you never let go of my hand. Walking briskly back towards the warmth of our cave. Never letting go. Your angry demons never surfaced at weekends. You buried your nose in my neck, and we researched, planned, speculated; sure of a future that would take us to Petra, Egypt, Turkey, even, maybe one day to Syria.

Sometimes, you told me about the scared and scarred boy, hidden inside, protected. You protected your core, now laid bare and open in my hand to nurture and love. I read you stories. You cried. You told me about borstals and prisons. You were in one way or another part of the young people under my wing. You were in them and so was I. And so, during our Sundays full of ice-cream and cake, we grew a new skin, protecting both of us. We learned to let go of secrets, of fear. We were safe in our new skin, our cave and our words. Or so we thought. During all of those Sundays, hidden and in silence, you grew a new core. Cells, eager to take over what you had protected and endangered at the same time. Unseen enemy, invited by you, when you still believed yourself to be invincible. You were always so proud of the healing power of your skin. Showed me, how cuts disappeared quickly, leaving only a smooth, beautiful surface for me to stroke and caress; the same speed with which cells, deadly, stealthily took you away from me.

Dark, without you there is nothing but darkness and cold. Our plans drowned in one moment during a storm. Your eyes will never water again in the wind. Ice-cream churns my stomach and tightens my throat.

Travelling with your Ashes

On the outside, somewhere not connected to me, things are planned. Not travels or adventures, but plans for you, your shell. The living decide how they treat their dead. And you have not written it down. Our plans, you have not written them down. I could tell them, allow you that last bit of grace. But I fail you, again. I am not blood, we, Us, don't count. Others decide, press you again into the world that was so cold and cruel to you. A world that was not yours and that you created, nevertheless. They take you away. In a cold van, back to crude voices and away from the sea. Back to plastic flowers and enormous TVs. Some try to talk to me, at me. Shout at the unreasonable me, who is choking on screams and crying tears where no fluid is left. Your angel sister calls. Her voice different and hard. They have told her that there is no money to bury you. You have not long left me. Not long enough for me to understand who we are now. I have run out of words, there is nothing left in me to defend you. I will find money, will pay for flowers and limousines for the family, which does not include me. I am not your family, not blood. I am nothing. Your daughter who worries too much, rings to tell me that I have to register your death. I am lost. Did not think it was urgent. There are schedules for formalities. Would you be any less dead if I miss the deadline? Will I keep you alive and next to me, if I just ignore the request? I have a deep-seated dislike for forms, records and declarations.

When, many years ago, my son was born, I could not bring myself to record his name. Five days were not enough to know him well enough to give him a fitting name that would be with him for all of his life. So, I was late at the office. Facing a bored, thin woman hiding behind a dusty desk filled with stamps and seals. Dark room, full of paper and files, holding lives, births and deaths and I wondered what would happen if I set fire to it all. Would all these people, born, married, dead, cease to exist? Are records not kept the death of truth and breath? I chose his name in his father's language. Farsi, ancient, poetic, full of flowers and scent. The thin woman consulted a book and told me that I could not give him this name. It did not exist in her paper clad world. And as I had waited until just before lunch on the last legally allotted day, I might have edited my son out of existence by not giving him a name. Confused, I looked at the small person in my arms. Too much responsibility. Mesho, meaning light, was unacceptable. Too foreign for this office, not recorded in any of the papers that mattered.

I chose another name. His father's name in French. And the name of the main church in my city. Tall, unyielding tower covered in green copper. Looking out over the harbour and Hanseatic proud people. The top of the tower now covered and protected with mesh against those who try to fly into another world. The woman behind the desk was happy, or at least satisfied. Typed the name, sealed and stamped and signed. Giving my son a name not connected with either of his cultures, but fitting into the book of rules that governs who you can be when you are stored amongst thousands of other captive lives. I imagine millions of pressed flowers held prisoner in volumes of dutifully reported events.

And now, in the here and now, that I can only see through milky glass, I have to register you. Missing soul, unfound, lost. I have to make an appointment, and someone will ring me at an arranged time. Again, it is a woman's voice, maybe females are somehow predestined to keep records and deal with confused mothers and wives. She has the paperwork from the doctor and the undertaker. Less to explain. Basic information. Strange words sticking on my tongue – deceased, passed away. She is patient, speaks softly. I know what she is asking, but speaking, finding the answers is impossible. She reassures, is kind and makes it worse. But we manage. Between us, we can establish and log that you are no longer with me. She is the first person, who uses that terrible word – I am no longer your wife. I am your widow. After having learned to be a mother, a teacher, a lover, an aunt to vast amounts of adults, whom I had never met before, I am now a widow. I have to end the call and rush to the bathroom. Sick, vile fluid leaving my body. A widow. What is that? Old women are widows. They sit in front of whitewashed Greek houses with blue doors, clad in black, with their hair covered. They grow geraniums and their veined hands pat grandchildren's cheeks. They jump onto funeral pyres because they have nobody to protect them. They accept and bow their knees in front of their fate. I need you to come back and tell me what I am now. Widows are to be pitied, accept charity and take a chair in someone's house, because they should not be alone. I retreat into my pillow mountain and try to find a spot, however small, that still smells of you.

I never believed in broken hearts, and I do not believe in them now. The pain lives in the middle, right in the centre of me. Cramping, bending over and endlessly screaming, the core of me. A heart is just a heart, a massive muscle, driving the pulse. Your pulse was the last thing to stop. At 19:54 the machine stopped, your soul left. My pain tells me that my heart in still intact, still working. My pain started, when your heart stopped. You believed that the core needed protection above anything else. Keep it warm, keep it safe, never expose it and you will not get hurt. And as we allowed our cores to merge, we made it possible for this unbearable event to take hold of us, of me. The others, your kin, they are organising, planning, crying together. Beating chests and tearing hair. Sometimes their own, sometimes each other's. The undertaker, a long way away, obeys the law. No matter who I am. No matter what you wished. Not my signature. I send things for you to travel with. No matter, not my decision to make. Our rings, you wanted them to go with you. On our hands forever. The Egyptians, the old ones, took servants and food. They took horses and weapons. They had a boat that would take them to the other side. Large enough for a whole court to surround them. Nobody would have dared to remove rings from the king's fingers.

My seafaring ancestors took offerings and weapons into the afterlife. Burned boats and sent them to sea. I have sent your fury blanket, just to keep you warm and the little silver statue, which had found a place just above our bed. A present for both of us. Lovers bending towards each other, their foreheads touching. When Aly gave it to us, you laughed. Impression, you said, of us dancing our way to the bathroom. I wish for one more of those trips. One more time, stumbling, dancing, giggling, painfully slow on our journey, but warm hands and foreheads touching each other. My own hands are the only thing now touching my shoulders. I walk on my own, against my will. I still stumble but cannot dance. I still make my way, back at work, I am sure I am talking, I must be present, but something stands between me and the muffled world. Screaming on the inside. You, on your own. Cold, whilst things are organised, flowers mutilated, and limousines selected. They never gave you the blanket or the little statue. They did not leave your rings, our rings on your fingers. They need money to pay for something you did not want. Or maybe you did. So many messages, so many words letting me know that I don't know you. Maybe you belonged there.

Every night, when we came home, we believed that you belonged here. After I found you at the station, you, some days more stable on your feet than others, walked across the road, onto the green. Without fail, you took a deep breath, held my shoulders and pointed at the stars. Home, you were home, where the air smells of freedom and salt. Sometimes, when the waves were high and angry, you challenged them, shouted, waving your arms. A duel between you and the gods of nature. And you were sure that you would win. Neptune had nothing on you. You were home. Your heartland, your happy place. Our place, our cave. Home in the Us. Did I know you? Or did you belong to that other world? Did you love me, or did you just want to escape? Do you, ultimately have to return to that dark place that made you unhappy? You often chose what you knew, because even in unhappiness, it was familiar.

I find myself at the end of the pier, staring at the river and the sea. Their tides merge, or, in reality, there is only one tide, cut in half, taking different routes. The land and the sea melting into each other. Benches with names. Maybe those of others, who came here in pain. The cold spray washes my face. Impossible to see, but the waves are loud and clear. They are honest and free. They travel and soothe. Come back, tell me that I knew you. Tell me that the Us was real and true. Tell me what to do, what is right, for you and for all of us, who now have to find our way without you. Come home, walk down this pier, give me any kind of sign to find the path. The sea, eternal, will be here without me, without you. It does not know me, and yet, I am part of it. Part of the wind and the water, part of this pier. My country is flat, with oceans on both sides. With beach baskets and boats. Gently rising dykes full of sheep, protecting the land. My country is the sea. The people, my mother's people, are strong, sturdy and harsh. They love quietly on the inside, their faces in the wind, fighting the storms. They plough, fish and tend cows. Everything and everyone in their place, fighting the soil and the sea for a living, not easily given, but earned, nevertheless. They sailed forever, finding new lands, but always returning to the harbours of home. The red bricks and solid roofs. Our houses are squad, strong, challenging the wind and the floods. They are built for cattle and people. The winters are long and harsh and the same roof protects everything living, separated only by the space used to store straw, boots and tools. My people return from their journeys to the warmth of the hay and the brightly coloured flowers painted on doors during the long winters. Their language, unique and older than so many others, still spoken by some. Not given to frivolities, they are thought of as cold and unfeeling. Dying in battle or at work, they go and drink at Freya's table. Strong bodies and faithful minds, large, useful hands and soft eyes.

So, how can I be so weak, so feeble, so pointless? I will not fight your children. I will give them what they ask for. No choice, one signature made sure of that. No choice, but to break my promise. To fail you again. My face, my hair, my skin, wet from the spray or from the water that will just not stop streaming from my eyes.

You owe me a doughnut, many doughnuts and 20 years. Neither can be claimed anymore. You owe me our life, our future. But I owe you more. I owe you to keep my promises. I have to make you matter, forever. You matter, you mattered, you were part of Us. You mattered in your own right and as part of a whole. I kept some promises, broke others, some are still to be kept. No hospitals, no bright lights or machines. You flew on the wind, free, painless and without fear. In our bed, under your fury blanket. That is the promise I kept. But I could not keep you warm, could not make sure that my offerings were with you, and I could not keep you here. My heart, my love, my part of Us, is here, waiting for you. And, my beloved, we will travel. We will be free and make the world yours. I will keep that promise. I will make you eternal, will write you down, paint you and keep you alive. I will be the thorn in the side of those who forget you. You mattered, you and your demons, your beautiful ears and your feet. And when I have completed my tasks, made every minute of your life count, I will come and join you. Because, after all, I have only promised to do my best.

Working, talking, fleeing into hidden corners, hiding so that nobody can see. Food, offered with love, grows in my mouth into boulders, sticking to the roof of my mouth. After work, I run back as fast as I can. Back into hiding. The cat, ever reproachful has not forgiven me for your absence. Not getting undressed, brushing my hair only when I have to go to work. Some think they know what I need. Everybody is still obsessed with me not be being alone. All I want is darkness. All I want is to go back, back to that moment. Or before. I don't remember your face as it was. Just the cold moment after 19:54. I want your old face, your smile, your breath. But, if I don't work, some say, I will have bigger problems. How can anything be bigger than no longer being Us? The milky wall between me and the world is growing thicker and higher. They think that I am here, that I listen and speak. But all I am is an imposter, a shadow, lost, weaving my steps carefully, so that I don't bump into the outside, don't disturb their clean lines, mapping out futures and hopes. You used your own medicine to render your numb enough not to remember. I have learned as a child to go to other places. No faces, no words, no beauty, just other. Did not need to close my eyes. I would stare at the fist and did not feel the impact that was surely to come. Never showed pain, never cried in public.

My head, my thoughts, me, we were somewhere else, where nobody could find us. Books. There have always been pages to escape to. Traveling in other people's lives, hiding in the library across the square. Just across the place where the market came every Wednesday and Saturday. On market days, I stared for hours out of the window, watching the seagulls feasting from discarded crates, whilst stalls were dismantled, folded and taken away, next to leftover tomatoes and cheese. The cart came in the late afternoon and crunched the thin wood, whilst the birds rested on the fences, waiting for whatever remains were dropped on the floor. I watched the seasons, watched the clouds and dreamt of a place far away.

They knew me, small, blue-eyed girl with short hair because that was more practical – they knew me in the library as well as the pubs. My mother, who kept a clean house and a civil tongue, would never enter a pub full of men. Too risky for a pretty woman with thick red hair. Drunk, noisy men full of dark words and false laughs. So, she sent me, four years old and for years to come. Ice-cream handed from the bar to keep my quiet whilst waiting. No laughter on the short way home. Just a hand in my neck. Hot, hop-laden breath full of threats and resentment. No visitors at home. Crisp white curtains to keep humanity at bay. Prevent them from talking and keep the staircase clean. Smiling at neighbours who pretended not to have heard the thumbs. Never scream, never draw attention. Clean shoes and a small voice. I never learned to be diplomatic. My big shortcoming, always pointed out by my mother whilst cooling the wounds, applying plasters and reprimanding me for not keeping quiet enough. My broken skin healed thicker and the other world stronger. Unreachable. Unprotected. My mother, cooling my wounds, which she later denied. I don't need to be numb, because I am too far away. You needed the bitter fluids because the pictures behind your eyes were too painful. And only the stinging in your throat reminded you that you were alive. Your darkness and my darkness were different and yet the same. And now, after the light, the warmth of Us, there is nothing again. Worse than before, deeper, darker black waves. You cannot miss what you never had. Had I never loved you, never met you, there would be no loss. There would not be this big empty dark space that has swallowed me and the world we created. I stare at the clouds and the trees, the stones on the beach. I need to find you. One more time, I need to see you as you were, when we were Us. I need someone to tell me that I am dreaming, that nothing of this is real. If things were different, I would need my mother. I would need her arms around my shoulders. She sends money and I have my books.

Endless calls and emails to the funeral director. Why are they no longer undertakers? A strange word, undertaker. Does it relate to undertaking or taking under? And really, they are not taking anyone anywhere. Even stranger to direct funerals. Do they have a running order, actors, need adjustments and managing? He is angry at my insistence, impatient with my requests. Conflicts, differing information. Lies. Confusion. I want your, our rings to go with you. I want you to have your fury blanket. But being edited out means that he cannot help me. I need to be the client. The only person that matters, you, is somewhere in a cold room at his place of work. You have no voice. And I cannot speak for you because I am not the client. I go and see your bank manager. If I pay, I might be the client. Strong, with steady hands, holding the certificate that confirms what the world should know anyway. You are no longer here. He is a young man with the beginning of a pouch and a bright red tie under a weak chin. Sympathetic until I cry. I cannot stop shaking, crying. Words, answers to his questions will not come. He seems confused and unsure what to do with this shaking, lost heap of humanity in front of him. And there, on his desk, under the bright light lay the two parts of my life. Marriage and death. 100 days apart, together, next to each other and unable to be reconciled. My hopes, my dreams and my nightmares. I flee, run. Just manage the signatures, grabbing my papers, I run. This is your bank, your money, not mine. I don't want to meddle in your affairs. But this might the only way to keep our rings on your fingers. In the car, I scream, wince. It is not enough for the funeral they want. Most of it but not all. It might be enough for me to become the client. To become someone who matters, who can make you matter.

I speak to one of your brothers. The one who escaped. He thinks me weak. Says, I should stand my ground, sounds like you. But the unreal pain in my glass cage is too much for me to carry already. I cannot fight with the outside, with your kin, your blood. And after all this, I am still not the client. The signature, that one moment during the night you left me, makes me invalid. And they say that I will not have your ashes. I can have what is left. There are so many of them. I researched the law, the rules that surround death. Nobody can own a person, but whoever pays for the service determines the rest. I have more rights to your possessions that your ashes. I can sue for the rings and the green t-shirt, but not for your dignity, for Us.

I need at least that; I need to bring you home. I cannot prevent the preacher, the flowers or the limousines, but I need to bring you home. Restless, I walk through our cave. Stare at the picture, the walls and the tree at the end of our bed. Cradle myself into your pillow that smells less and less of you.

I stare at the laptop screen- you disappear, disintegrate, right in front of my eyes, the pixels, the fragments of pictures and words. Your Facebook page slides away and is gone forever. You had some things planned and laid out, had forgotten others, have left me in a hostile place. They, your kin, have your phone. I gave it to your youngest, with trust, to make calls that I was unable to make. Did not think, consider, that now all our messages, hundreds of irrelevant tales of late trains, missing each other, dinner requests and plans, were now laid bare. Accessed by eyes that thought they had the right to enter our world. The world that was just us. Privacy no longer relevant or respected. I am not your blood, not your kin. One night, you made a decision, took steps. You made me the administrator of your Facebook page. From the moment, when we became Nothing, you wanted me to be your caretaker, your voice. You told them, but they could not hear you. And your youngest, again, thought she needed to take the reins, take control. With your phone, she took the power to invalidate me, Us, you. She took your phone, your password, Us and changed your presence in the cyber world. And now you are disintegrating, right in front of my eyes.

Because she is not me, she does not know, had not been given permissions and the responsibility that weighs so heavy on me, some algorithm destroys, disables and closes your accounts. In my status, I am still married, but no longer married to you. Your presence erased, vanished. Your digital footprint raked away as if taken by a Japanese gardener ordering pebbles. I flee into the wind, onto the beach.

Photographs, wedding pictures, blown kisses. Sitting on our wall, low, facing the sea. The last place we walked to. Across the road, the green, a little uphill. You and Mick, next to each other. Your cheeks hollow, your eyes bright. You were so proud, holding onto my shoulders. We made our way, to this wall, low and cold in the early spring sunshine. Me, frightened that you might lose your footing. You, determined. Whispered into my neck – we will see the spring. We will see my birthday. You will see, my queen, you will see, and we will make next spring. And I wanted to believe you. But Mick's eyes told me different. Our last walk. No longer proud, sliding and gliding as if you owned the earth. But not fumbling and stumbling either. Shuffling, holding onto me, but determined, nevertheless. And arriving, swinging your leg over the wall. Smiling, your beautiful smile untouched. I wanted to believe you. But now you have gone, somewhere out of my reach, out of hope and presence. Your strong, slight body in someone's place, who keeps bodies for a living. Your, our history fallen away. I can no longer look at your pictures, your messages, because they have been erased, removed from the unfathomable cyber sky that seems to have clouds, but nothing that can survive when the wrong button is pressed. I shudder, another death, another loss. How many times can I lose you and not fly with you? Sick, bile seeping into the pebbles, washed away by the tide. Heaving, my insides in unison with the sea. Crouched on my knees. Tell me what to do. Don't send me feathers or rainbows. Tell me what is right for me to do. Tell me where you are, where you want me to go. My hair, matted and wet, soaked in vile fluid and salt, clings to my face. I cannot defend you, cannot protect

Us. I am weak without you. I am weak, lost, a mass of bleeding papercuts. Your past taking revenge on me because you are no longer available. You have left me with your demons, but no weapons to fight. Before you, I was strong. A turtle's shell around me, always ready to retract my vulnerable neck. Always running, traveling, moving on. With you, I was strong, soft, opened like an oyster to love and the world. Forming pearls from our fears, growing into hopes. Now, I am a pile of bile on the pebbles, because I have no space for food anymore. And all I can see is that moment, when you dissolved into pixels, falling onto the bottom of my screen, without any way to catch them. And the moment at 19:54, when your eyes were not closed and not open and the pulse on your neck just stopped, leaving me in silence. On my own, on the pebbles, shouting at waves that don't know me or care about Us, but are always my home. Always the place I run to. In every country, on every coast, never standing still for long enough to leave a mark. Lost in the sea and the dreams of the other coast, that might bring peace.

Travelling with your Ashes

At the end of the pier, staring at the river joining the sea; Sheri and Kelly, steadfast, reminders of life, friendship, mine, theirs and ours. We laugh at the seagulls and search for doughnuts. I cry quietly, picturing events as they happen miles away. Now, at this moment, your kin, hair and nails groomed to perfection, enter limousines. Solemn, worthy of the occasion. They are going to take you, in some hard, wooden coffin to the house you left, swearing that you would never see it again. And follow you, sure, confident, righteous and amongst themselves. When you dictated the list of those you wanted to be with you on this last road, my name came first. Me, your wife, the remaining part of Us, broken and lost without you. Without the strength to fight hoop earrings and fake pearls. They took my will and my believe in Us, in love, in you. Your son, the one born before you came along, already there when you moved in - like me, not blood, called last night. In secret. The others in the house, he at the end of the garden. Away from the hate and the anger. He wanted me to come, after all, he wanted me to come. He would face them with me, he said. You loved me, he said, and that I would regret it forever. I sent a daffodil, just one stem. The ever-surviving spring. I sent a poem. A last message to you. I hope they, after all my pleading, left your rings on your hand. Our rings, our pledge. I have a link on my phone. Could watch the speeches and the grand displays of grief. But I sit here, at the end of the pier, with nothing but love for you and our friends. Each of us secretly watching the clocks, thinking of events as they might happen. No doughnuts, too early in the season. Seagulls and sun reflecting back onto our faces. You and me, we often wandered over these cracked planks of wood, separating the beach from the river. We laughed then as we laugh now. Staring at waves or stars, eyes watery from the wind. Watching children crabbing and dogs running through sand at low tide. And your hand always in mine. You did not like the cold and I kept you warm. You held me back when I was leaning too far over the black railings to see something small and glittering in the water. We smiled at Andy, my friend with the camera, taking up his post at the end of the pier to capture the sky. If you are there, maybe he can find you and bring you back to me. Why do we always assume that souls go up? Why the heavens and the stars and not the waves or the fields? But now I cannot be with you, if indeed what is left now is still you. I hope your beautiful soul does not need that broken, cold body. I hope you are free. Please remember me, wherever you are. Did you love me? I know I love you.

Another funeral, many years ago. My fragile, small grandmother. Finally free from the pain of this world that did not understand and that made no sense to her. During good times, she took me for long walks, taught me to see berries and blooms in the snow. Taught me to make juice and feed me toast. In her small flat, with windows leading out over the windmill and a small garden. During her good times, she let me listen to the sea, captured in an old shell. We laughed at the mice, eating her medication from the kitchen table. Mice from the attic next to my bed that had been my mother's. Bustling during the night, making me feel safe and alive. During the bad times, she cried, shrank into corners, pulled plastic bags over her head, ran in front of cars and left no pills for the mice. A shadow, my ethereal grandmother with her hair black until the end. I brushed that hair, long and thin, wispy until it was tamed into the knot at the back of her neck. Screaming ghost of herself. Visiting her in a strange, cold hospital. Her eyes broken, her spirit in a different place. Me, four, maybe five years old, before the birth of my sister, staring into those eyes looking for my grandmother, the person I trusted the most. But she was gone, not for long, just for now. She would come back they said. Taken away by some wires and electricity they said would her happy again. I don't think that she was ever happy, even during the good days, she was sad. Hospitals, more bad months than good weeks. A little more lost every year, a little less able to breathe every day.

They were talking about her, as if she was not in the room. As if her confused, lonely mind could somehow not understand what they were planning and organising without ever asking her. Poor woman, they said, with her wondering mind. She sat in corners, with her hands folded in her lap, looking at me, the small girl with the short hair and blue eyes, looking for comfort. My eyes held her, before I knew that she needed holding. We both wanted them to stop talking. Stop throwing words into the air and thinking that her body needed to live, when her soul had no strength left. She took my hand and we quietly slid into the kitchen. She knelt down, held my face. She asked me, not to despise her, like the others did. I did not know the word but could never forget that moment. And I promised. I wanted her soul to fly, be free, as I want your soul to find a peaceful home. They wanted her to live. A prisoner of breath and words, chained in darkness, which in the end would not lift anymore. My beautiful, small, shadow of a grandmother, finally escaped into the hospital garden, during the night, half naked and drowned in a pond, in shallow water.

At her funeral too, they gave speeches, a pastor, who had never met her, never felt her pain, quoted some verses. I remember my anger. My great rage. They had failed her, hidden her behind pretty words of empty hope. Many years before that moment, they should have let her fly away, into the light. Her sadness engulfed her world and the little girl at her feet deserved better. Dignity robbed. Life lived too long. Others deciding what was right. Less guilt if she lived, no remorse needed because they kept this body alive. Even that day, I knew, that I should not have gone. Should not have drunk too much before arriving at the church. My anger, greater than me could not find words. And my mother's red eyes, full of relief pleaded with me to accept and leave. I could not bring myself to follow the coffin, left before the dark soil swallowed my tiny grandmother and the coffin that was far too large for her.

And now, at his moment, at the end of this pier in a different country, my pain does not find words. My friends, chosen family, helpers when carrying the rocks of pain on my shoulders, hold me. And I scream into the sky and the waves. Behind my eyes, there is only the picture of your pulse at 19:53. There are only your half open and half-closed eyes. This time, on this day, my pain is greater than me, a giant crushing me onto the wood of the pier.

This journey, 16 weeks after that day in spring, I cannot make on my own. Incapable of thought, frozen and driven with fear, I sit next to Sheri. I am shaking, staring ahead, trying not to imagine what might happen when we arrive. Unable to protect you, defend Us, prevent that they took you back, I have grown sickly and small, timid and confused. I avoid to make noises, want to be invisible, unheard, unseen, unnoticed. Finding dealing with kindness even harder than dealing with the hate of your kin. Hoping every night that there might be no morning. Existing in some reality that I am no longer part of, unable to reconcile the two worlds that I inhabit. The reality of others, where I work and breathe and talk and the shadows where I am looking for you. Trying to understand why you are no longer here and what my purpose might be. Walking next to others, sitting on benches and the pebbles, I know they are there, but somehow there is a milky, dark wall between me and everything else. The wall only lifts when I am on my own and can think without interruptions of you – recalling your pulse. Your pulse, that did not fade, but simply stopped A clock, running out of seconds and minutes. A calendar, pointless, no longer counting days or years.

We are on our way to Croydon. To meet the undertaker or funeral director, or celebrant, I cannot remember. They have collected you from the crematorium and some oversight of your youngest allows me to collect you, bring you home. After weeks of fighting, of studying the law, misunderstandings and collisions of different universes, I can collect you. Can bring you back to the sea, our home, to

Us. I don't think I am heartless, unfeeling, unable of understanding. They are your children and that they have rights. The right to keep your death certificate in a frame over some imagined fireplace; the right to decide what should happen to you and where; the right to keep your phone and read your most private thoughts and of course the right to your things. I would gladly give them all of your things, if I can just bring you home. I did not attend when they paraded your through Croydon and held their speeches. I did pay for a coffin and flowers and orders of service you did not want, just to earn the right to become the client of the undertaker. Immaterial, like all other of my attempts to protect you. Misunderstood, like your brothers' efforts to save what was important to you. Weak, I am weak and feeble as I sit here next to Sheri, scrutinising the houses we pass, wondering over and over again, how people can flourish in this dark, grey place. And yet, this had been your universe for most of your life. Survived without ever breathing real air or lying in grass, watching the clouds. Threading your way through the throng of people and rubbish, through mistrust and raised voices, instead of books and the sea. Candles on cakes, but never in windows. This place, imprinted on you like one of your tattoos, unable to feed your soul or to look after the little boy hidden deep in your core, has claimed you back. I retch, remembering the day I took you home to the sea. Shake because I don't know if they will be waiting for me, with their harsh consonants and broken eyes. Sheri steers us safely, unwaveringly towards you. The undertaker's offices are locked, we have to ring a bell. Death by appointment, arranged grief. I am not sure what I expected, but the girl with the white trainers and the tracksuit takes me by surprise. She is friendly, talks about her children, the cost of school uniforms and the numerous emails between us. Apparently, the funeral business has done well recently. I am not surprised, pandemics and old people are good for undertakers. Less scared now – they are not here, they are not trying to stop me from taking you home. We make conversation. The girl with the white trainers disappears into the back and returns with a purple velvet bag. So, this is what is left of you? Your son with your name refused to carry the coffin. Thoughts flit through my brain, like lightning, unconnected to anything or each other. Flowers, preachers, your children, hoop earrings, chest pounding, you alone and cold and tears all mingle and concentrate into one big bolt. My eyes are hurting. She hands me a very small black bag. Stiff velvet. It contains your wedding ring. They have kept our engagement ring, to give to their mother. I stare at the ring, at the girl with the tracksuit and Sheri. I need to escape. Leave, leave now. We exchange more friendly words, and she expresses some kind of regret for all the trouble that has dominated the last few weeks. Apparently, death brings out the worst in people. I cannot concentrate on her words, stare at her lips. I need air. Carrying your urn to the car, I am surprised at your weight. You were slight before, where hardly existing at the end. How can you be so heavy now? I cry on the way home, but I am relieved. I am taking you home, back to the beach and the books, back to safety. Home, I am bringing you home.

Travelling with your Ashes

Carrying you down the steps to our cave, I cradle you in my arms. You are heavy. But it is not just you in the urn. There is also the wood and the handles, and I do hope that my lonely daffodil went with you. Although I think they take handles because the don't burn. Do they use them again? I know that they did not give you your furry blanket, nor our rings or the little statue of two small people holding their heads against each other. Those things are lost forever, somewhere where they no longer matter. Somewhere, under the metal lid, carefully placed in purple velvet, there are your bones, your skin, there is, somewhere everything I need to be happy. But they cannot have burned your soul. Tell me, please tell me what you want me to be, what you want me to do. I need your soul with me, next to me. I need your feet searching for mine at night and I need your hand holding my fingers in the car. I am glad, grateful, that I have this, this velvet clad version of you, but I miss you. You as you were, your words, your warm skin. Can you see, from where you are? Do you remember Us? I want you to be somewhere we you can see me, protect me, never leave me. Some say you do. But, if you could see, how would you feel about everything that has happened since you left? And as much as I want you to remember me, remember Us, I don't want you to be sad. It would be unbearable to think of you somewhere, missing what we had here. Maybe the missing is just for the living. Maybe you have found unlimited freedom. If there is another place, I want you to be in the right place. Not a place that might judge you by what you did, but who you are.

And you are beautiful, a mass of contradictions, helpless and cruel, a victim with many victims you have created. Lost in a world governed by shrill voices and pain, a bird of paradise in hell. My husband, part of Us, now broken. The little boy at your core, the hidden one, I wish peace for him. The peace you only found when it was too late. Have you travelled through the hall of Maat and has Anubis weighed your heart against a feather? Your soul was innocent and light, I know this. Your deeds were not. But surely, they only weigh the soul? And your soul was light. You cannot have gone with Freya, you did not die in battle, did not hold a sword. Or have you crossed the Styx into the darkness? I don't want darkness for you. Not the darkness I wade through, trying to find you. No, I don't want you to be with some vengeful God. I would wrestle you back. I need to keep you alive, your soul, your essence, need them alive.

Everything happens for a reason, at the time that is set. We believed that. But all belief is easy when my head rests on your shoulder and we release words like butterflies into the room. God has left me, the universe has taken you and left me as a black crow on the beach, trying to build a nest from dreams. Scrabbling and scraping for pictures and truth. Alone, with cold feet and a churning stomach. Sleepless and hopeless, bound by promises. Do I really have to keep my promises if you did not keep yours? 20 years, you promised. Mobility scooter races and nights on the beach, you promised. Roses for anniversaries, poems and treasures, you promised. You will not be here for our first wedding anniversary. There will be no flowers, or candles. 'Till death us part', you promised. And it did.

I sit in the corner of the sofa, with you next to me. Staring at the urn, I remember my promises. 'You have shit to do', you had said when I said that I wanted to come with you. I have no idea what that might be. I promised we would travel. I promised you would see the world, explore the ancients. They had kept us company during the pandemic. When we had time, unlimited time. When we lived through historic events, we explored the humans before us. We researched past pandemics and speculated about Atlantis. We had Us, the cat and the fish. Making plans. And then, later, I promised that you would travel. That I would meet your mother. That I would write you down. That I would give you a funeral in a woven coffin with daffodils. I have failed, could not keep you here. But I have brought you back. And we will travel. Your grave will be the world. Every ocean will know you. I have written you down, vomiting words for ten days. I will plant daffodils for your mother and feed bees for both of you. Your mother, confused, fragile mother, taught you how to feed bees. A little sugar, some marbles, water in a beautiful bowl. We fed bees and remembered your mother. I never quite understood why you were not angry with her for leaving all of you when her mind wandered and she had to go away to be made better, with you and two brothers having to look after the little ones. For not defending you against the violence and pain. I shake your wedding ring from the small black pouch. Pain, unbearable pain rises in me. Our engagement ring, why did they keep that ring? Yours, ours, the real moment of our pledges lives in that ring. We became one with that ring, in that moment, in Arundel amongst the dust and the coins on a rainy day in the spring. With the seller of coins as our witness, with the universe's blessing, we pledged future and past. We gave souls that we did not know we had until that moment, when you gave me a woven silver band with some crystals, and I gave you the Irish worry ring with the moving middle. And with the biggest grin of your life, you ordered ice cream. You never had ice cream in February in the rain. And we thought we could have many of those. Grey skies, fine rain over the cobbles, with the most decadent ice cream in our hands and our rings, we were one. And then death did us part, and that ring has gone. I have your wedding band. Flat and silver in the palm of my hand. I love you, no more or less than on that day. My ring now next to yours in my hand. I am not sure what to do with yours. Some people lock them away, other wear them on a chain. I only ever wear my cross on my neck. I cannot lock it away. It was meant to go with you. Both rings were supposed to melt with your bones. Suddenly, our wedding rings slide into each other. The fit perfectly, my ring in yours. So close that nobody would know that they are not one. Seamlessly, the fit into each other. And from now on, I will wear them both, welded together. Strength. They will give me the strength to honour my promises. For now, I sit in my corner and let the tears stream.

You are home and sometimes I can sleep. Not for long, not deep or refreshing, but I sleep. With the urn next to the bed, my dreams are calmer. I travel through the rooms with you. Wherever I go, I carry you with me. I have to make decisions. Eventually I will have to open the urn. There are endless messages from your children. They want what is theirs, what you have promised to them. Each of them you promised a bit of you. Was there some fear in you, that they might forget? I cannot bring myself to unscrew the lid of your new metal home. And yet, this is not you, I am reminding myself, unsure what you are and what is in that urn. For now, I will visit your mother. I have to find out where she is. I ask your brother-nephew. The child of your eldest sister and yet your brother; left with your mother, who could hardly care for the children she had. You grew up together. Somewhere, your ways parted and then crossed again. He is the only person who can tell me where the grave is. The only one, who visits it whenever he passes through on one of his journeys. When you wanted to take me to your mother, but could not even walk to the bathroom unaided, he went to see her. Stood in for you. You wanted to believe that we could go. For some reason, you needed to go to that place where you felt the worse of your pain. You tried to arrange that someone would take us. When your mother died, you broke. You had spent years, three long years, trying to keep her cloudy, confused mind in one place. Cared for her as you never managed to care for yourself or your children. In the end, her soul forgot how to breathe and grew wings. Death brings out the worse in people, the girl with the white trainers had said. Weddings and deaths bring the broken together and shatter the pieces into even smaller shards.

You never recovered from the pain, from being misunderstood, cast aside, blamed even. You had siblings, a feuding, disembodied clan. Each of you misunderstanding all others, each of you damaged in different ways. And another story of hate, mistrust and revenge began. Broken, alone, you kept away from the circle around the grave, when they lowered your mother into the earth, as you had lowered her into her bed every night. Stayed away, apart, alone. You did not belong, not then, not before, not ever, until you became part of the beach and the sea and tentatively tended new, vulnerable roots. You only once visited that place again, much later. And then you found that your siblings had finally managed to agree on a stone and had it placed at your mother's head. You found the temporary marker, a cross with a small brass plaque in the grass nearby and took it back to your room. The only thing from your past. You had no pictures, no reminders of anything or anyone. Just that cross and your mother's purple dressing gown. You had brought it to my house, the small cottage, where tiny rooms flowed into each other as they would do on a longboat. In the morning sun, the pine of the cross glowed golden in the corner of the room. And you, with your back to the to me, stretched into the light. Healthy, happy, your skin smooth with a small dimple at the bottom of your back. I knew you were smiling and that the cat would be waiting for you in the kitchen. Coffee for me, watching you dress and not minding that I would not see you for the day. I knew you would come back, to some station, depending on luck and timetables. And now I have to find your mother's grave alone, without you. I know which cemetery to visit, and I have a grave number, I also have your angel sister to help me. Everything in this world seems to be numbered, registered somewhere, ordered. As we park the car, it suddenly occurs to me – this might be where they took you, held their last bitter speeches. Your sister, clutching flowers for your mother, nods into the thick air. This was where the limousine stopped, where they placed the flowers spelling your name.

A hot day and I have come to the place where you were transformed and transferred into the urn. We are searching amongst the stones and the high grass for a small number, telling us that we have arrived. She cannot remember where the grave might be, or anything about the gravestone. I call your nephew-brother, he seems to be as lost as we are. I have to make sure that he does not know that I am not on my own. People, your kin, your feuding clan, would not understand, why your angel sister would help me to find her parents. The grass, higher than my waist, hides your sister, but I know that she is trying hard to remember something that her fragile mind is hiding from her. She remembers being here, she remembers seeing you standing a long way away from the mourners, who had been unable to tend to the living, but played their part on the day of ceremony and duty. As you played yours, separated, segregated, unwanted reminder. Probably drunk, probably dry-eyed, leaning against a gate until they all had gone. Your sister and I search amongst the leaning stones and the hight, dry grass. No flowers anywhere, no signs of any human visit for a long time. Quiet rest, untouched by memory or living hands. Most of the letters, engraved once deeply into the stone, now shallow and faint, eroded by time. We search for a long time, without any sign of our destination. In the end, we stop, sit down and decide to come back during the week, when there might be someone in the office. I take her home, confusing labyrinth of roads, houses, busses and unpredictable people.

And so, I make my way back to the beach and the air. To a place where the sky is larger and higher, wider and clearer. As I turn a corner onto a smaller road, fewer houses, more trees, two lanes, my stomach churns, heaving, trembling. The road we took when I collected you; the last time I was on this road, we were hurrying towards our future. You fell asleep along this stretch and did not wake until we reached the beach. Drunk, hopelessly drunk, stowing your few belongings into the car, you could not wait to arrive home. The rain made the journey hard, but despite being asleep, you never let go of my hand and I felt safe. Safe and happy. Now, despite the sun, despite the clear road, I feel sick. My hands shake, pulling over to the side, I just make it out of the car. Heaving, shaking, a stone boring itself into the middle of me. A fist, a rock, a boulder, pounding my stomach, my chest. Unbearable pain, realisations. Not understanding what has happened but knowing that you are not next to me. You are not holding my hand, your fingers are not entwined with mine, two wedding bands on my finger and I am vomiting into the verge.

Travelling with your Ashes

And so, one day, unremarkably in itself, and even if it had been remarkable, I would not have noticed, I take the urn from its purple, velvet cover. The velvet, stiffer than expected, respectfully and coyly covering the metal that holds what is left of you, folds down neatly to the middle of the urn. Your picture, our picture, taken on the day of our wedding, 100 days before you became a shadow, larger than me, larger than anything else, sits in the middle of the table, next to the urn. My hands are not shaking, the promise I have made to you steadies my fingers. The lid is harder to move than I had expected, maybe a sign that I should not open it, at least not today. Maybe on another day, we, you, I, are more prepared, ready for the moment when I have to face whatever there is to discover. My face is wet, and I wonder if I should have asked someone to be with me. You, me, Us, We, are doing this on our own. Only you are not here to hold my hand, steady my breath. Your skin is no longer looking for mine. The pain in the middle of me, the me, that is nothing but a collection of mad atoms that have disintegrated, makes me double over, holding on tightly to one of the little necklaces, you and I had chosen.

Days, months, years ago. Time, immaterial as air. The cat saunters in. The cat is real. Since you have left, he has become restless, requires relentless feeding. Does he miss you? Does he understand? They say that cats can see things, know things, sense and feel more than we can. We are staring at each other for a while, and I lift the lid. I am not sure what I expected. Not sure how I expected to feel when I saw you again. Hoping you would talk to me, say something, give me something to hold onto, something to understand. The ash is light, nearly white. Somehow the colour is wrong. You are dark, surely this white, oily, powdery substance cannot be what you have become. This cannot be you. But what are you now? What is Us? If you have become part of everything, why can I not feel you? If you soul still exists, where is that place? Where do we go? Can I come and find you? I have always found you. You often took wrong turns, wrong trains, missed connections, left late, fell asleep on trains or picked the wrong carriage. I never turned the engine off when waiting for you, full well knowing and expecting that you might call from another train, another station. Waiting for me at some place unknown to you, misplaced, misdirected, lost as only you could be. Chasing from Arundel to Ford and from Ford to Barnham. Barnham, where the trains go to die. And so, I found you, drunk, lost, small giant of a man, in the middle of the road, daring the traffic to fight you, watching out for the car, for our safe space, for me to take you home. Your face, hardly visible, tense, tired, split into your familiar grin. Happy, caught by the headlights, warmed, found, rescued, safe. Keeping you safe. And now I cannot find you, feel you, hear you, I have nowhere to look for you. All I have is this urn, this picture, these small pendants, my shaking, cold skin, shrinking away from the ashes. Shrinking away from allowing my brain to make this our reality. Us in an urn. Us on this table. This might be our last moment alone. Just you, me and the cat. You are still complete, some people believe that you need your body in that place that is After, some think the soul can only fly when the body is burned.

They did not burn your rings, our rings. You always said that these rings would never leave your hand, my hand, they would go with us, wherever, whatever. You said that you wanted them with you, on your hand. And yet, they took them, as they took you. Your tattoos burned with you, someone else's name on your hand. That was with you in the end, in those flames that I see in my dreams. The flames, hot, hungry, uncaring and cold, not caring about souls or what is left behind, turned you into what you are now. They blended skin, tattoos and your Dr. Spock suit into a grey, grainy substance that is all that is left. They took possession of you as your kin did. They devoured, swallowed and changed you. You, who could never be owned, held, chained; you, who was restless and free in the chains of your pain – they took you when you could not protest and even snarl anymore. They took you back to the place you never wanted to go back to. Did they burn the flowers with you? Ostentatious blooms, pressed into letters and words, at £50 a letter and with your name being long, there were any of them. Did they burn the daffodil with you? The one, single stem I sent with one of your friends. The one thing reminding of us. I am sorry. I have failed you. Twice. Could not keep you safe, could not keep your breath in that body of yours, unable to stop, to halt, to prolong any further the ultimate result of the hurt of your life. And I could not keep you here, where you found home. I could not stand up to the claims they made. Kinship, blood, longstanding past, memories blurred and pressed, twisted and shaped into a picture that fitted and befitted, that was suitable for each of them. Me, You, Us, edited away. Immaterial, insignificant. Surpassed by greater pain, by older wounds. My wounds are young, grew out of a thousand paper cuts that in the end made your shape. And when I found you, we found Us, my wounds were healed, the shape in me filled and complete. And you gave me the frightened boy, the unruly youth, the runaway man, the drinker, drug-taker, gambler, unfaithful blind searcher. You gave him to me, tentatively, cautiously, but completely. And I promised to protect him. Not just for you, but for me, for Us. I needed him to be safe, to stay in that shape in the middle of me, that was void before you, before Us. What is left now cannot fill that shape, cannot replace us, leaving me with painful edges around the hole, with the thousands of papercuts bleeding again, open, as if every one of those injuries were fresh. Boulders of memories, bound together in no particular order, forming rocks, rolling, cascading over me. My face, wet; I don't cry. Tears ceased whilst I was young. I don't cry. I don't wail. That is not me. Strong, unbending me, dancing only to my tune, never quite hearing the chorus right. And yet, I have done nothing but crying and wailing since you left.

Wiping my eyes, I fill the first little vessel. Small, shaped like miniature pineapples. You loved them. And as we could not make you into diamonds, they were the next best thing. And small black obelisk shapes for the boys. I fill them. First recoiling from touching the ashes but growing determined and more sure handed. Steady. Filling 24 tiny necklaces. Placing them in small sacks, grouped into the different parts of your tribe. With letters for each of your children. Your kin, your past, your blood. Even if some of them where not of your genes. To you, they were your clan, that you should have headed and led. But you ran, did not cope, abandoned, caused pain, returned and cut more wounds. I write in your voice. That is all I can do, give you a last chance to be heard. And most likely, as during your time of breathing, it will be misunderstood, misread. But, my Darling, I manage this first task of many; seal the box ready for someone to take it away.

And so, one day, today, without purpose or plan, I take my running shoes from their shelf. No longer able to stand where I am. Quicksand under my feet, reaching up to my chest. Choking in pain and tears. Screaming through nights and floating through days. Old wounds bursting and nestling in fresh ones. One more time, let me hold your face one more time. But you grow fainter. Unreachable, gone. Where are you? Out of my grasp, taken by your demons. Malicious devils leading you to me, only to take your breath and my life.

Staying is hard, impossible. I am a nomad; you are a restless soul. I must find you. Must show you all the things you could not see. You did not have the time, the chance, the will, the belief to see. I will take you. Invisible you. Whilst running, I will show you the world. I will make the globe your grave. I am your tour-guide, your undertaker, your memory. I am your eyes, your ears, your legs. You will be a traveller, never arriving, staying in parts, staying behind to guard our memories of Us. You will be part of everything, and you will be everywhere I go. I will leave you behind and make the globe your resting place. I have to start at the sea. The sea outside of our cave. The waves you shouted at and that soothed you. Behind the green. You will sail, will find the place you wish to land. No flowers or speeches, no confinement in a coffin, you will be free to dance on those waves and let the wind carry you. I buy little envelopes, too small even for dolls-hands and matchboxes made from buff cardboard, and white feathers. And construct your little boats, the ones that will carry you safely to whatever your destination might be.

Randomly, I select a date and ask people to join Us at the beach. Our friends, my chosen family and your Liberty family. All of those, who travelled with us during those 7 weeks towards the end. Some have attended the other funeral, the service with the preacher and your kin. And now, I need them to celebrate your freedom and your beautiful soul with me, counter the bitter words your daughters had for you at the other place, their last revenge, the final word.

Filling every one of the small envelopes, writing my love in tiny letters on the stamp sized paper, crying over the white feathers and making a sail, I realise that nobody, who has been visiting you, crying over your breathing chest and assuring me that they will stay in touch, as actually answered my invitation. Nobody has looked for you in my eyes. Nobody has asked what happened to the shadow who made their tea and held your hand. They have found someone else to book lorries and vans, to share their breaktimes and wait until the last Friday night drinkers have gone. Someone else at your desk. Living and breathing. Maybe they talk about you. And a new bitterness rises in me. I know, nobody owes me anything, no obligations, to ties of friendship and past. Yet, somehow, every visit, every promise, every coffee is invalidated. Especially those you thought to be close to you and the one I trusted enough to ask her to write down what you wanted to happen in the After. They ought to be here, to share this moment, when you enter the waves; but they closed the chapter of you at that other please that was not you.

I close your boats with red ribbon. You will sail, my Darling. I study the tides. On a Sunday, under a grey British sky, we will let you go for the first time. Celebrating you, missing you, setting your sail on cardboard boats the size of matchsticks. You mattered, my Darling, you mattered, you were my Emperor. And if some have closed the door in that cold, dark hall at the cemetery, you will still have left an imprint on their souls. From time to time, they will remember, I am sure. And I hope they will smile.

Your guests arrive, I have left my corner amongst the cushions, need to move, organise and stop myself from imploding into a myriad of little pieces of tears and salty wind. Once, on a day in December, when you were tired but fine, not an inkling of what might be our path, in a corridor in Crawley, when we promised each other a lifetime, we had made a plan. A party at the beach, with everyone, without giving a reason, no presents, no speeches, we would celebrate the rings on our fingers, which would stay for all eternity. Today, we will have our day at the beach. Without holding hands and maybe with speeches. Without your arm over my shoulder. I have studied the tides; I grew up at the sea. I understand tides, high and low. Mick, Jenny, Sara, Jo and James each holding their little sailboats. Each of us with our own thoughts, the others watching me closely. I can feel their eyes on me and try to shrink again. Try to disappear into the shadow of your boats.

James is the first to speak. I have studied the tides, I am sure, I have picked the right moment, the right place. And yet, today out of all days, I made a mistake. You, your guests, and my shadow, amongst the pebbles at low tide. The water will come back later, you will not sail into the open sea as I planned. I can feel you laughing at me. Your humour and my tendency to turn disasters into adventures. Seven of us, in a circle at the edge between pebbles and the sand left behind when the sea retreated for a rest from the land. And we cry and we laugh. Only you could sabotage this moment, take solemnity and turn it into a farce. If there ever might be a sign of your presence, you would choose this. You would don your joker mask and laugh, turn my sombre plans into a moment of amused confusion, with your shoulders against the wind, you would smile.

We bury our little boats in the wet sand, only the feathery sails showing, hoping that eventually, when the tide turns and covers your boats with water, you will set sail at your own pace. Without spectators, without tears, you will make your way across the dark, salty expanse.

We sit on your wall, our wall. Mick cries and James, ungainly and lost as ever, still holds his boat in his hands. He will not let it go into the incorrect tide. James, with his faded red hair and freckled arms, who was your landlord for a few months, my friend for years and yours for as long as you knew each other. We met once a week, the three of us, whenever he was in this country, and we argued, laughed, discussed and sat in absolute silence. The two of you, like small boys, planning pranks and looking for ways to disconcert those you had offended you with superior airs or fake smiles. The two of you, observing the world, each coming to his own conclusions and trying to make sense of the senselessness of humanity. James is now standing here, unmoved, unruffled, still, holding his little boat. He will meet me here tomorrow night, under the full moon when the tide is right and we will let you go as you deserve. We will battle the wind again and discover that your voyage against the storm is impossible and that your small boats keep returning to the shore.

And James will find a white feather on the bonnet of his car, which is further inland and smile wryly into the sky.

The lake, not really a lake, more a hidden pond, nestles under trees, amongst brambles. The water white, milky and green, turquoise, reflects dead branches and stillness. Today, my Darling, I am taking you to one of my most secret and sacred places. The path onto the Downs from the village is steep and sandy, overgrown and one of my foraging grounds during the blackberry season. Today, my Darling, I show you the water that appears to be milk, solid fog collected in a small basin amongst the old forest and just a few steps from the open fields that are the home to wild grazing cows. I will take you to the place that I visit often, where I can sit, far away from noise, even the birds hush and the ducks dive silently. I can sit with my small book of memories and search for your ghost above the surface of the water. But there is no ghost, there is no you. I wish I could believe in ghosts, in souls returning, touching the shoulders of sleeping lovers. Searching for the memory of your face, before it became thin and drawn, when your skin was soft and firm, and before your cheeks were hollow and your eyes, too large, hovering above sallow greyness, I dig my fingers into the inside of my hands. I am trying to remember my hands on your neck, your smile returning mine and the gladness we had. Further and further away, I try to capture that memory of your face, the shadow of us, how we once were. But all I can see is what came later, at the end, just before I grew into a lonely crow, left in a nest of thorns, unable to fly and too restless to stay. I will bring you roses, will bring them here. Maybe this is the one place I can visit to bring you gifts and thoughts. For this journey, I have built a special boat. A letter, white feathers, the envelope with you nestled warm in your matchbox sized boat. Your sail is larger than usual, I found a peacock feather. Peacocks, the birds of shahs, of kings and emperors. Royal and proud, not very bright, they march on their paths without ever caring about obstacles or people. Versailles, ostentatious, overblown and too much of everything, was nevertheless home to white peacocks, glowing against garish human colours.

We are far from the sea. No storms to keep you awake and no birdsong to sing you into your sleep. You are safe in the chalky water, amongst the branches and the sky reflecting on your feathery sail. Carrying you, my emperor into the middle of the pond, where eventually, I am sure, you will sink. For a second, I am glad that you are here, amongst the enormous roots. Neither of us ever had the time to grow roots that would hold us in one place. Anchored in the familiar, solid, nourishing roots to keep us in place. Trees are as eternal as the sea. They die, the burn and if they are left, they grow fresh shoots from old roots. You and me, Us, we were the results of too many cultures, too many traditions and languages that seem to cancel each other out, leaving a void, to large to fill. Sometimes I feel speechless, lost one language and not having found another. Unable to find words to explain, to describe. Words to package the rocks on my shoulders and leave them behind for a while. How can I describe you, your demons, all those beautiful facets of you? The prism of your essence that I so often wanted to capture and hang into the window to marvel over it in the sun. The love that for most of your lifetime you could neither feel nor receive? How can I describe your cruelty, your warmth, your need to hurt yourself, the clown, the thinker, this other part of Us? How can I capture a sinful saint with a crooked smile and the pain that was scattered along our path until we finally arrived at Us?

I watch your small boat float slowly, deliberately into the fog. It is time for me to go. I don't want to watch you sink, want to remember your boat, with the proud feather. If I cannot remember your face as it was before you shrank, I want to remember this. I make my way into the open field and stare at the clouds, as I so often did as a child. As I lie in the fog on the damp grass, I can feel the cows passing on their way to the water trough. They are used to people, but do not need contact, assurance. They wander past us small creatures with the air of a patient host, who will reclaim his home as soon as the visitors leave. Watching the sky and the clouds, slowly drifting and seeing faces and castles and ships in the changing sky, I feel small and safe. And maybe, just maybe, I might find you.

When we lived through the historic event that was a blessing for Us and kept us at home, together, warm, awake and curious, we fell in love with the ancients. Ancestors with unknown genetics. Closer to the earth and the trees and maybe even to the stars. We explored, debated read and made notes. And later, I had a plan. When we began our journey towards the storm that took your breath; when your pulse was still strong. When there was an illusion of hope. I had a plan. All organised. We were going to take you to Stonehenge. Two hours from our basement by the sea. Surely you could manage two hours. Surely with all our love carrying you, you could manage. We had friends, who were going to help. All organised, only a date to be set. But, like most of our plans, my surprises, my hapless and hopeless attempts to show you the things you deserved and craved; that intrigued and kept you alive, it shattered on the 25th of March. We did not make it; your rogue cells growing faster than my hastily assembled ideas.

And so, our first journey away from the sea will take you to those monolithic stones, that incomprehensible, inexplicable circle. We had theories, differing, arguing, but in utter agreement in our admiration. Both wanted to touch the history hidden in stone. I had touched the monoliths once, after a long muddy walk across fields, many years ago, when I could still feel wonder, and butterflies left me breathless. Before mobile phones and a lifetime before you. Sheri, Kelly and I set off. Me in the back to hide my tears, clutching the small glass bottle in my fist, my nails making the inside of my hand bleed, opening the wounds I have punched into my skin ever since you left me. Pretending that you are next to me, laughing. Before the pain, the diagnosis of Nothing and that stormy night in March. Before loving you enough to stay behind. Before making promises that are nearly impossible to keep. Promising to hold on, to set one foot in front of the other. Promising to take you around the world. Promising to write you down, to make you immortal. No grave for you. No stone with your name. A traveller on the wind, washed away by the rain. I feel hollow, excited and somehow purposeful. Our first journey. To the biggest headstone I could find. We leave in the rain, dark, grey, contemplating the walk through the mud to the stones.

And as we arrive, the sun breaks through the clouds. Shines and warms like a message from you. Is there a heaven for you? Has the God I am angry with, and you did not believe existed, accepted you? Can you see us? Do you know about my pain and the confusion you caused? I shake myself, in the hope that the thoughts will fall off like water from the pelt of a fox. I stare at the building, large, unyielding - a badly designed bus station in a beautifully soft landscape. The new gateway to the stones. We pass through, with others, too many others and find that there is now a bus to make the way easier. No wading through mud, no chance to bury you quietly and in private under a stone the size of a small hill. Suggestions on signs indicate how to take pictures from different angles and there are ropes around the Henge. Guards in heavy yellow jackets watch closely. I am not sure if they expect someone to shoulder one of the neolithic giants and take it home. For you this means that you cannot rest under the stones, the ancient circle is barred to our ritual. All henges are round, not all are majestic. But you wanted to see this one. We were meant to walk around it, through it; together. We were meant to lie in the grass and feel small, whilst speculating about purpose and method. But you would have been sad. No chance to touch the stones, whisper into a gap. Imagine whatever these people, who came so long before us, had done here. Rituals, not burials, maybe marriages, or praying for heavy crops, good fortune and appeasing their demons.

My purpose is clear, but not easy to fulfil. Leaving you as close to the circle of mystery as I can. We debate the legality of my plan. But there is no doubt in my mind that I have to fulfil my promise, that I have to leave you here. Even though you would have been as disappointed as I am and would not have wanted to stay in this place of sanitised magic, I have to make you part of this place. So, Sheri and I lower ourselves into the grass, still slightly damp from the rain of the morning. We are trying to create an impression of people posing for pictures, whilst internally working on our stealth mission, to somehow transfer you into the ground. Two women, no longer young lying on their stomachs in the damp grass, bending green blades to create space. Why do we seem to become more visible when we are trying to be inconspicuous? No longer cold in the strengthening sunshine, I have to smile. You asked me to do this, to travel with you, to show you the world and leave you at all the most important, beautiful places, but you never promised to make anything easy for us. You and your wicked sense of humour seem to stand in the way of making our journey a smooth and easy one. Finally, during a break in the never-ending stream of tourists, we manage to remove the corks from our small bottles and easy you into the grass. Exhausted, I am utterly exhausted. Turning onto my back, I wonder if those before us had to hide their intentions, if they were wondering about legalities and acceptability. Surely this does not count as a crime. We join the human throng again and wonder how small the stones really are and feel even more disappointed when we discover that some of the boulders have been fortified with concrete as they might otherwise have crumbled away. The crows, or ravens, I can never tell the difference, are obliging and take fruit directly from human fingers. They hop, ungainly and comical. Black feathers gleaming; beaks carefully picking at red, juicy pieces. Conveniently, there is a fruit seller a little way down the small hill. Crows can carry out seven tasks in the correct order. They are the scientists of the skies. You knew a lot about birds. On our walks inland, you pointed them out and named them for me. If reborn, I am sure, you would be a bird of prey. Once again, I am grateful for the pandemic, the event we did not foresee, but that freed us to explore the past and sketch out the future.

Another failed plan of mine during our seven last weeks. I know people who have birds, large elegant predators. We had planned and schemed to get you to their place and see, stroke and fly a falcon. And earlier still, before we replaced long journeys with dances to the bathroom, we had hoped to fly falcons in the Arabian desserts. Now, the three of us, fulfillers of your dreams, feed black, shiny birds in front of ancient stones. We take the bus back to the misplaced building, housing a shop and a restaurant. I have a slightly bitter taste in the back of my mouth. The magic, replaced with concrete and aircraft hangers does not do you justice and I am glad that you have not seen it. I can no longer imagine druids worshipping the sun or some other wonder amongst these stones. But the birds, keepers of mysteries will guard you as you rest in the grass and view the landscape. I know that I will not return. Outside of the complex I find some thorny bushes covered in cotton shaped spider webs. Beauty away from the destination still counts and I leave a little of you in these intricate homes designed to capture food. Somehow, I am glad that you are here, amongst the thorns and the dew caught in silk.

 And with my heart full of birds and intricately woven nets amongst thorns, heavy with love and pain, we return home. Back to the place where I can still find some of your smell and your shoes are still where you left them.

Travelling with your Ashes

You left me in the spring, amongst hints of early sunshine and daffodils. You did not see my Easter tree or the first camelia blossom. Your feet did not glide over the warm sand at low tide. Not this year, not ever will you wake again to a season of hope and unpredictable rain. My old restlessness has returned. My companion, propelling me into the wind and the waves, into the storms, recklessly searching for nothing in particular. I am crying less, screaming on the inside, leaving only a void in my face, uttering words that seem to be generated by a part of me that is more instinctive than real. Here, my Darling, I am back in Croydon, at the cemetery. I have found your mother's grave. In the end it was easier than I thought it would be. One email to the right people and they were able to send a map. The rectangular plot, smaller than a single bed, is unkempt and unloved. Nobody has been here for a long time and the grass has claimed the earth. The large clan of her children listed on the black, shiny stone.

I sit for a while, quietly watching a magpie. Industrious, purposeful and with seemingly endless energy, this much maligned bird collects nesting material. Dismissing some twigs and choosing others. Holding them in its beak, returning some to the ground, until the perfect building block has been found and selected. The bird returns to the tree, where the other half of the pair is waiting; both of them now placing and weaving their treasure with determined care. How do they select, chose, know, which material is the best for that particular part of the construction? Black and blue feathers glitter in the sun. You and I would wonder and marvel at these small, hidden moments. Your mother used to watch bees. Taught you to feed and love creatures, small and thirsty in the summer. I feed ants, enviously watching their strength and determination, whilst I feebly remove the grass and overgrown weeds from the grave. The winnings from your lucky dip collection, which you assured me would provide me with comfort in my old age, have given me enough for two rose bushes. One for this place and one for our small garden. I plant the rose, hopefully yellow and red, when it eventually flowers, lavender and bulbs for next spring. The freshly dug earth cascades through my fingers, leaving my skin rough and dirty. I leave one of the small bottles in the void under the stone. The magpie is taking a rest, or the nest is finished to perfection, either way, both birds are now sitting amongst the branches. Me, the intruder, they ignore. I should not be here, this is not my place to care for, to visit, to be seen. This is a place for your kin. But you were desperate to take me here, for me to meet your mother. And I promised to go on your behalf, to look after this small patch of earth. My gifts to your mother are the pebbles I brought from the sea and the plants that will cover the earth and feed the birds and the butterflies. And I brought you, to remain under her headstone, to whisper all that you never said whilst either of you still had words. Your mother's confused brain would not have heard, and you did not have the words, not then. But you found them, during our time in the cottage and later in our cave by the sea. You found the words and the peace you needed to form them. Love is not jealous, love is kind and gentle, it does not anger easily and forgives without thought or hesitation. I remember quoting this verse, one night in the cottage. And you stared at me for a while and then broke into your glorious grin. You held me and for the first time in your life, your demons slept and purred. You found the words, found the space to feel and to be. The boy, hidden and scared, lay in my hand in your words. His words, the child's pain, crying, weeping and being held became the building blocks for our nest by the sea. The magpies are resting, your mother's small garden in restored and I return to the sea; on my own.

I have researched, made sure and confirmed, and yet, I am uncertain. We are on our first long journey. You are travelling on your own across oceans and on the wind, but now we have to cross borders, have to board planes. Negotiate security and controls. You and me, me with old demons on my shoulder and weak knees, you, nestled in small glass bottles, covered and safe in a red bag. Next to you your paperwork, just in case. You will not need your passport, I have all the certificates that might be required, and yet, they might tell me that you cannot come with me. Might confiscate you. I promised you travel, and I will do everything I can. At the security gates, I declare you, believing it to be necessary. My hands shaking, head spinning, I can only hope that they understand. The man behind the conveyor belt in his neat uniform looks slightly confused and bewildered. But it is not you that he cannot understand. He wonders why there is so little of you. Apparently, it would be more common to bring a whole urn. We agree that so little of you does not need to be declared, certified or documented. He asks, if I want to take you with me on my person or if you should go with my things through the x-ray machine. I think you would enjoy travelling through the machine, that is not designed for people. When you had a body, when you were with me, we waited too long for the machines to examine what was happening on the inside of you. Maybe, if I had insisted earlier, if we had wondered, examined and paid attention, you might be here, with me, holding my hand, steadying my spinning head. Bought us coffee, pointed at planes, kissed me, looking forward to leaving. Instead, I collect you, together with my toothbrush and dresses at the end of the line. We have managed the first part of our new obstacle course.

I find a seat, staring at the departure board and marvel. In the life before you, long before you and even before my daughters, my world had shrunk. Shrank until only I was left. My body would, could not walk outside of the house. Three years inside, unable to manage even the garden gate. Long years of convincing myself that there was no reason to face the world, confusing and large. Loud and glaring. The world came to me, working from home was easy. Telling myself that I was fine, was easy. But in the end my prison became too small, and I learned to walk again. Beginning at the garden gate, feeling my way to freedom. Learning to accept the frozen legs and sickness, the dizziness and aching muscles as phantoms of shackles created by me. Learned distraction and strategies. I still struggle when crossing roads, noisy places and bright lights are to be faced head on as major challenges. And yet here we are, my strength in small bottles, in memory of you and your hands. The promise I need to keep and the shadow of Us steady me. Our first journey is going to take us to an unknown place. A place I would not have ever considered, even during my traveling days, long ago. But, lack of funds and the certainty, that James will meet me in Tirana have made this our first destination.

Watching the clouds from above, I wonder what it might be like to walk on them. They look surprisingly solid and sturdy. We are now really on our way to explore. And we explore together, the unknown, hoping to find beauty and places where you would choose to stay. The last obstacle might be the border, with more checks and questions. But, in the event, the officials welcome us to Albania, and we find our way to the exit and James, who is waiting for us. James, watery blue eyes and freckled skin, wearing his ever-present hat to hide his reddish hair; our friend, is waiting for us in the hall and we step out into the cool dark night. Taxi drivers argue with each other, there seem to be people manning everything that is dealt with by machines at home. They check tickets, take money and open barriers. I am searching for familiarity in the language, but my exhaustion numbs my ears and, in the end, I let the words wash over me. We make our way away from the airport, sidestep Tirana and head towards Durres. The motorway is lined by ostentatious buildings, bathed in light, that create shadows to hide the smaller structures amongst the columns of hotels imitating Greek palaces. Broken beauty put aside and overshadowed by glare and shabby pomp. Staring at the beach and the twinkling lights from James' balcony, I wish you were really next to me, standing behind me, holding my shoulders and show me the stars. I wish I could point at the boats out at sea, with you breathing into my neck. James, always unsure how to respond to emotions, hands me a tissue to wipe my face. You and I made it. Through Gatwick, corridors and checks, through the boarding and disembarking, through passport control and my fear. We have made it to this point, this place. And I will find the most beautiful places for you to stay.

I slept, finally, for a few hours. Ready for coffee and the beach. Our first morning reveals the sea, tankers idling on the glittering surface of the still water. The waves are tame, small, gently whispering against the shore. Nothing like the wild, spraying, gashing ocean I know so well. Neptune at ease. There is a gap, where a building once was, created by an earthquake, not long ago. And I can see the water and the beach. Tall hotels, marbled facades and more columns block the rest of the view. Today we will walk, and I will find a place for you. The first place for you in this country, that does not seem to have numbers or names for houses, not even for most roads. You will decide where you want to be, James will guide us. He will show us the beauty of his chosen country and help us to navigate the tears.

James will take us to a place above the sea, hills full of olive trees and undergrowth. I am impatient, the sun is strong and promises heat. And so we set off, smaller and smaller roads, winding into the sky. The earth is dry, parched and yet gives birth to an amazing array of fruit. We leave the car in front of a high, shimmering construction, somewhat akin to a chimney or an industrial vent. Stainless steel towering over a low crouching building, filled with faded prayer mats. The path is stony, dusty and steep. We pass an absurdly modern house, small, grey square concrete. The weathered woman in the garden stops chopping wood and greets us. She wants to know why we are walking. People in the middle of nowhere do not walk without reason. James explains something, which is greeted with some head shaking. A flood of incomprehensible consonants later, he translates that the woman is sad because her son has left for Italy seven years ago and is yet to write. Her house, her farm fell victim to the earthquake and her son was not here to help. The villagers have helped her to construct the shapeless concrete cube that is now her home. And still her son has not written or send money. More words fly through the still air. It appears that she has asked why I look so sad. James again, explains on my behalf. He explains you, how you left me, I am sure that he is not telling her that you are in my pocket to remain in a place overlooking the sea. Suddenly her eyes rest in mine, some shared understanding. Husbands die, their souls fly away and leave women like us to chop wood and face the wind, waiting for letters from somewhere. A sisterhood of sad women.

We continue on our walk, which quickly turns from a walk into a hike over stones, steeper and steeper, whilst the path itself grows narrower. Designed for goats, with thin, steady legs and a sense of balance far greater than mine. We negotiate our way, climbing, sliding, crossing ridges just wide enough for one foot, until we reach a small plateau. The sea shimmers in the distance and the view makes my breath and my heart stop. Can you see the large ships we saw this morning from the balcony? They are now minute flecks in an endless expanse of water and sky. You will never tire of this picture of perfect, endless freedom. Maybe the wind will take you into the sky and you choose another spot. But you will never leave this view.

You once dreamt of building a house for us, on a hill, overlooking the ocean. And you turned and woke me up, excited and happy, describing the house and the small garden, the dogs and the sheep we were going to have.

Nothing seemed impossible, apart from this moment, when I set you free in the Albanian hills, leaving you behind, alone, without me. You will not need a house, a place to keep you dry and cool. I will not give you a stone to mark this place. You are free to wander and settle wherever you wish. And I am bound to continue to walk through a life I no longer want. At last, we continue our stumbling climb, holding on to sturdy vegetation. I cannot understand, how these thorny, low bushes can cling to life on this barren, clay filled earth. We manage, somehow, to make our way into a valley. A small stream guides us to the bottom of the gorge, green and cool, whilst the skin of my legs brushes against thorns and nettles, inflicting small bleeding wounds. I wash my face and we speculate, which direction we should choose. In the end, we decide to trace our way back; the makeshift mosque serving as guide. I am tired, my eyes holding on to the tall, silver tower in the distance. Sometimes it appears to come closer and a minute later it feels unreachable. My hands, already punctured by my own nails grapple with thorns and rough sand. I am aware that my feet are larger than the narrow path allows. And yet, James stumbles and I manage to keep my balance. The sun is unbearably hot. But still, I can breathe, freely and unafraid. I feel the earth and the stones under my feet and my hands, breathing new life into my skin.

A few hours later, we finally pass the widow's farm. She has changed position, hanging out washing. Her son still has not written and she is sad for me, for us. Her eyes, buried deep in her small, oval face, bearing the landmarks of a life, too long and too lonely, are brown and kind. I know that James declines coffee, some words do not need to be understood to make sense. She waves as we turn towards the path, less energetic than we were in the morning, probably still pondering about the sense of walking into the hills and climb with the goats.

A donkey stands next to the mosque, not tethered, still wearing a cradle on his back. He dozes in the heat, his head slightly bowed, from time to time lazily flicking his ears to chase flies away. His sad face looks tired, and I wonder why donkeys are always sad. Sitting next to the grey animal for a while, in the shadow of the silvery tower, I take another small glass bottle from my pocket and leave you here, in the care of an unknown god and a tired donkey, in the hope that the villager's prayers might help you on your journey and somehow sustain and protect you.

The light on the water and the horizon is golden, with specks of purple and orange. The sun drowns slowy in the horizon, melting into the rippling water. Somewhere behind me someone plays guitar and sings. Something between a call to prayer and the sad songs of the gypsies. James plays with our friend's children. They should not see me cry. This is our sadness, yours and mine. I sit, a little away from people who take pictures of the glorious sunset, with my feet in the water and you in my clenched fist, wondering about this perfect moment. It is perfect, peaceful, still, and yet, hollow and does not touch the tears that make me choke and my eyes blink.

The truth, my Darling, is that I pay the price for your addictions. The small, lonely boy at your core, the one you gave me to protect, was alone, soft and unsure of the world. But he had to be covered with layers and layers of skin and pretences. And pretending for you was easier in a place of numbness. When you were drunk, or high on whatever could enter your body, you were supremely confident. A clown, a joker, jovial, charismatic pretender. You covered your wounds with distractions, with gambling, cards and horses and strange games with women. Shy exhibitionist. Always making others hurt you, so that you could feel something. Pain for you was the only reality, until you found words and peace and someone who would always wait for you and bring you home, only pain and emotions the size of volcanos could make you feel alive. The amber fluid, the pills and the powders made you believe in yourself. But, in the end, they took you back into the rabbit hole, where there was no escape from the pictures burned into the back of your heart and scarring your soul. And here I am, a lonely, abandoned crow with her feet in the sea and you in my hands. I slide down a little closer to the water and let you go. In your small glass bottle, you make your way towards the sinking sun. You sail on the glistening sea and I turn around and join James and the children, who have a whole life still to come.

The man with the limp, one leg shorter than the other, calls me Madame and speaks to me in a curious mixture of English, Albanian and Italian. He believes me to be from Italy, I cannot correct him. Maybe James will tell him. Here seems to be a general assumption that I am of Roman descent. Strange really, considering that my people were not conquered by the Romans, despite their best efforts. My colouring makes it impossible to stay invisible in Albania. I discover that I can make people stop and stare at my eyes. And as it is not really an Islamic country, I cannot veil. The restaurant is dark, full of pictures and objects with no obvious purpose. Trinkets, pictures and dust mingle in the warm air with a drum-set in the corner. A few women work in the kitchen, cleaning, re-arranging, smiling, whenever they pass me.

Whilst James and his friend play, working out harmonies and songs they both know, I wander back. Back to a time before you, before my children, before anything. Before my skin split into lines and gorges. When time and money were insignificant, and the world was nothing other than a big playground for my demons. Mikis, the oldest music venue in my city. Full of music, smoke and retsina. Posters, the piano, nicotine-stained walls, deep conversations that nobody could remember the next morning. A time, when I could juggle two trays on high heels. Working through the nights, surrounded by other night creatures, we would sing for each other. Family, closer than any other group of people I knew. One suffered, we all sang sad songs and drank ouzo. One finally got a paid gig, and we all sang and drank more ouzo. Paying customers until midnight and then the musicians, the poets and those who were just lost. Then, before I had even left school, the dying began. Hoddel's liver failed and he drowned in his own blood, Asher followed his partner in crime not quite a year later, Igor died on his own in a psychiatric hospital. Nobody knew what happened to his parrot or his balalaika. Bernd went to Munich and died soon after, still wearing his rabbit fur coat and enormous sideburns. Dimitris returned to Greece and Hammed decided that he had been an illegal for long enough and fought for a German passport; Wong went to sea and his postcard from Malaysia reached me only many years later. And still, we were happy, sang and drank more ouzo. We sat on the stairs leading down into the smoke and music filled cave, with balalaikas and saxophones, not caring, who would hear or could not sleep. Rushing home in the early morning light, changed and arrived at school just in time, I carried the smell of ouzo and warmth with me. Sleeping through Latin and Maths, but my teachers knew that I would wake up eventually and disturb their lessons with questions. I had so many questions, there was so much world to understand and discover. We read Bukowski and

Sartre, discussed and debated, called for action and demonstrated. Somewhere in some storage place, there will be my parka, still smelling of teargas and lemons. And whenever the sun shone and there was neither school nor work, we made our way to the nearest motorway, raised our thumbs, and travelled as far as we could. The girl, who was me, smiles at the woman I am. She is free and her wounds are still open and young. James renders Country Road and the here and the now mingle for a minute with the there and then. Had I known you then, would you still be here, still be with me? Would our children still talk to us? Would they have been blessed with your skin and cursed with my hair? Or does everything happen exactly when and how it has to happen? Did we both have to build spider webs of scars around us to find each other? Did you have to go just when you found peace and me being left without any purpose and without you?

I can feel my feet growing restless, run, I need to run again, away from memories and you. From your last breath and the small bottles in my pocket. We leave and walk along the beach. James asks me a strange and yet pertinent question. He asks how long I will travel with you. Will I travel until there is nothing of you left? Will I stop when I have taken you to the most important places? I am not sure. There is no answer. I will travel with you forever, but how long will you be cradled in small bottles and left behind? How many graves will I make for you? How many places for you to inhabit and for me to remember? How many times will I break the tissue trying to cover the wounds? How many times must I try to let you go? The truth is that I cannot let you go, fly away for the final time. I need you and I need to keep my promise. You matter, you deserve a whole globe. Different stones, different types of soil and water. Deserts, snow, mountains and sea, I will make them yours.

Albania is the country of doors, bunkers and plastic bottles. Sitting in the early morning sun, James and I make plans for the day. We are going to visit an Amphitheatre in Durres and a museum in Tirana. I am still marvelling over my cappuccino, served four paces away from petrol pumps, whilst smoking a cigarette. Smoking men cross the forecourt whilst filling their cars with petrol.

 Away from the beaches, there are no mock Roman columns and just past the slippery marble floors in front of the hotels, plastic bottles, wrappers and other unwanted leftovers form small mountains along every road. I can hear you laughing at the bizarre buildings, that could be half demolished or half built. Some have no walls halfway up a tower block, with occupation obvious in the upper and lower floors. Overblown pink villas that have never been finished stand next to crumbling houses with beautiful collapsing roofs. The most impressive feature of most places are the gates, strong, forbidding, designed to deter and keep the inside hidden. Doors, Albania is full of fascinating, beautiful doors, with their peeling paint and rusty hinges. These doors have weathered, seen innumerable years and storms. In the old town, just behind the glitzy shopping streets, I caress doors, tell you about them and take pictures. Hundreds of doors divert my attention on our way to the Amphitheatre in the heart of Durres. Just past the mosque and the square with the water features in front of a pink ice cream parlour, an insignificant, steep lane leads to the entrance. Buildings around the theatre teeter dangerously close to the edge. Balconies overlooking the theatre and the town, shutters closed against the sun. A meteor crater of history amongst a living, bustling city.

You and I would have been happy in one of these balancing houses. We might have repaired the peeling plaster and filled the balcony with the geraniums. Of we would have just left things as they are and sat in the sun. A long way to go for the boy from Croydon. A brown dog with white ears lies in front of the ticket office. Why do dogs always want to lie in the sun, even when the heat is beating down on them and makes them pant and uncomfortable? Whilst James buys the tickets, I talk to the dog about the strange ways of dogs and although he seems to be unsure of my words, his tail pounds the hot dust and he turns over for me to scratch his belly.

After the glaring sun, the tunnels under the theatre are cool and slightly damp. Small alcoves are covered with faded mosaics and frescos, beautiful like aged fabric and clearly not depicting Roman gods. Crumbling steps lead back into the sun and the vast area, covered with weeds and grass, surrounded by stone terraces. I sit for a while, watching the middle-aged woman, who seems to be employed to collect rubbish, mainly plastic bottles. Like a bird, selecting suitable nesting materials, she picks through items, approves of some, which she adds to the contents of a large bag, and dismisses others. I would like to ask her how she makes her choices, but she is too far away from my stoney seat, and I am not sure that she would understand me anyway. I have so many questions for this country and its people. So much to discover and understand. You, next to me in the sun, always worried about my inquisitive nature that makes me climb over builder's fences and into tunnels. But you promised to break me out from every police cell I might find myself in. Somehow ironic, that now, when you can no longer rescue me, I am probably committing more offences than ever before. Some of our destinations do not approve of people leaving human ashes at their monuments, their holy sites. Who will rescue me if I really face arrest? Maybe you are somewhere, watching over me. I wish I could believe that you can see me, that you are somehow protecting our journeys. But you have abandoned me, alone, wandering around the world. For a moment, just for a short, fleeting moment, I feel anger. Why do I have to stay and pay the price for your decisions, for your past? But then, the moment passes, and I feel the sun on my shoulders. Under my knees, there is a small hole in the stone. I open your glass bottle, the cork cracks slightly, and I sprinkle you carefully into the crevasse. You are now a part of a long history, found your place amongst emperors and peasants, overlooking whatever fight or games played out in the vast round.

Tirana, the capital of Albania, has welcomed us with open arms. It is cooler than in Durres, the architecture, however, contains the same labyrinth of the half-finished, over-polished, decomposing houses. For the first time, I see buildings from the communist era. Reminiscent of East Germany once upon a time, utterly lacking in personality or even plaster, some streets are lined with grey, crumbling blocks of flats, which I am sure, are damp and dark on the inside. They make me shudder, remind me of Croydon, of the darkness, the hopelessness of the living expressed in bricks.

The museum, for some unknown reason is closed, but James shows me the back of the building. And there they are, the old heroes. Two statues of Stalin, Lenin, who seems to have lost one arm and the inevitable young, athletic health fanatic, who was also loved by the fascists. Albania's past put aside, hidden behind a museum, but not discarded. I wonder if they kept these overpowering figures just in case that things might change again. There was a time, when Lenin was my absolute hero. But heroes invariably disappoint when their power and our experience grow. They fall, stumble over their own humanity. Not kindness, not all-embracing love. They trip over their power. One regime replaces another as occupants of grand houses and the holders of ample food change their flags, not their appetites. Turning the world upside down only rearranges the view, it does not change what is there. I once believed that revolutions would create justice and a better way of living. Spent hours and days debating, taking action against injustice and quoted Lenin and Trotsky. Fought against water cannons and rubber bullets. Became part of the wider movement against nuclear power, occupied a church after one of our number had been arrested. Protested against the Shah, because we did not know that the alternative would not bring freedom. Socialist principles and values were surely going to bring equality and progress. My trusted parka and I travelled through Europa to be heard, to change the world. Sit-ins and blockades, chants and leaflets, discussions with police, bending over their shields and presenting them with flowers. We were on a coach to some demonstration somewhere when we heard the news about Harrisburg but did in truth not prevent that I had to keep my son inside years later because of an accident in Chernobyl.

And then, one by one my comrades turned into unrecognisable insurance brokers, lawyers and supermarket mangers. T-Shirts with the red smiling sun became an acceptable fashion accessory. And now I am staring at the obsolete statues of the icons of my youth, the pride and certainty, misplaced and misguided. The principles of humanity and equality still strong, but the reality of daily living for most overshadows the memory of noble causes. We used to discuss politics, with you being proud of my convictions, without ever committing yourself to anything but surviving somehow. Maybe you were right all along. You spared yourself the disappointment of your heroes' frailties and the injustice they inflicted in name of their ideology. I will not leave you here, amongst the outcast dictators, placed, where nobody can see them.

James shows me the bunker museum and we enter the dungeons under Tirana. Bunkers, the old dictator was insecure and frightened, building bunkers in various sizes, but all shaped like cheese domes or concrete igloos. This one, large, dark and disturbing, recalls the past, the suffering, the pain of the Albanian people. Dictators, whatever their background or ambition, are the same all over the world and these pictures and cells could have been those of Germany's past. The air is full of fear and betrayal. The walls have absorbed the screams and pain of those who debated and wondered. Guilt overwhelms me. Ideals become monsters when the turn into reality. Once, when I was the young girl full of righteous anger, I thought I knew all the answers, now, as the wandering crow, I am not sure that there is anything left I can believe in. I will not leave you here, in this collection of personal hells. You were right all along. Survive or die, it makes no difference to the world. And all the change I can make and bring to the world is through my work. No more loud shouting and flags for me. Because when the shouting and the flags succeed, there is still more suffering, just for others.

I need to escape from this place and I can, unlike so many before me. The sudden sunlight blinds me as we leave the bunker and face the imposing Italian buildings that serve as public offices. A policeman smiles at me and my blue eyes, less startling than in Durres. We walk slowly, thoughtfully to the large square in the middle of Tirana, where I find a place that is fitting for you, between a mosque and a clocktower, surrounded by pigeons and in the shadow of Albania's hero, Skanderbeg. Not a very Albanian name, a hero on a horse, watching over you, resting between the faiths and far away from the sadness of a dark past. Suddenly, I feel exhausted, my bones, my whole body wants to shrink into the warm earth, melt into the small heap of ash. I am not strong enough to survive without beliefs and purpose, without you, without Us. James stops me from stumbling and leads me back towards the shabby part of the city, with its fragile, tumbling roofs and decaying doors, where I can breathe. We arrive back at his house just as dark has settled over the country. James sees something and beckons me to the side of the building. And there, amongst thorny undergrowth, discarded plastic bottles and rubble left over from one of the building sites, I stand in the middle of a swarm of fireflies. Blinking tiny stars, flickering in the dark like the spots I see when I am feeling dizzy. They never stay long in one place and my eyes have to try hard to catch glimpses of this wonder. I am breathless and awestruck, glued to the spot, until the air grows cold enough for us to make our way into the building. Beautiful, invisible creatures dancing just for you my Darling, and just for a moment I feel blessed.

Leaving Albania is harder than I expected. I have made friends Ledja, Erin and their three children, the girls, small Frida Kahlo copies, spirited and untamed; the stone seller who has sold me an overpriced, but beautiful necklace and now waves every time I walk down the road towards the coffee shop, where they remember me and have even found decaf coffee, which is waiting for me in the mornings; limping Illir in his restaurant with his frustrated musical ambitions, and of course you. I have left you behind in places of beauty and significance. But I will come back, return to this country of contradictions, where simplicity and pomp, poverty and richness of spirit, past repaired with concrete and unfinished, unplanned futures exist next to each other. Picking up bits of Roman pottery and unceremoniously throwing them back into the undergrowth is just a continuation of history. The beauty of doors and sunsets mingles with Italian villas and endless heaps of plastic bottles. A country where smoking in petrol station cafes is encouraged and the pavements are raised to prevent cars from mounting them to avoid traffic. A country with swallows, vast expanses of marble, and donkeys dozing in the midday sun. I will return my Darling and visit you in all the places you rest and you will tell me about the people passing you, who are unaware of your presence.

I arrive in the late evening and Sheri and Kelly are waiting for me. How can I describe what I have seen, the endless sky and soft light, the mountains and the sea? How can I describe the old man, who needed a lift to his house, which was not far away and who held his axe and his bags tight on his lap whilst climbing into the back of the car? His weathered hands plying us with the largest, sweetest grapes I have ever tasted. And his genuine disappointment when we refused lunch in his house as payment for a drive that took less than five minutes.

But, for now, my Darling, there is another task, the last of this journey. You and I became Us, when me met. Here, at this airport, at this spot, at the smoker's corner outside the arrivals hall. From that moment, there was Us, with surprising ease and terrifying speed, we grew into this new being that is now wounded and halved, with the gaping hole you have left. Sheri and Kelly stand guard, block me from view as I crouch down on the dirty pavement. I gently let you glide from your glass bottle. You blend surprisingly quickly into the uneven paving stones. My eyes sting. More significant than any other moment; I have returned you to the place where we first found each other.

Back in our cave. Safe, I should be safe, and yet my eyes sting, my whole being screams. I light your candle in the window, pointless, but strangely comforting. My hand rests on the urn, the lid cold and solid. I cannot do this my Darling, I just cannot put my feet in front of each other anymore. My aching body cannot travel the world, just to keep my word. I am tired. The razor blade in my other hand reflects the flame from the window. There is nobody to hold my hand to keep me strong, there will be nobody to close my eyes. Nobody to look after my body when, one day, it will break and give in. Nobody to search for my soul as I am searching for yours. Restless, like a caged animal, I wander around the flat. Our home, our nest. Your jacket still hangs over the chair in the hall, with your shoes neatly tucked underneath. I should dust or move them. All my life, when the scars were hurting too much, or when lost dreams drowned in my screams, I cleaned, dusted, re-arranged. Picked fresh flowers, washed windows and curtains until exhausted, I had to sit down on the bottom of stairs to stare into nothing. You will not be coming home tonight, will not notice the new bedding and the gleaming windows. So, I just stare at nothing in particular. Before you, all my life before you, I did not know that I could love. Unconditional, unquestioning, just love. We did not need to change the other, our imperfections bleed into each other and painted a new world. We did not have to chain each other; from the freedom to leave, came the freedom to stay. Just love. Neither of us were prepared, after our respective journeys over twisted paths and boulders that had to be overcome, to find this absolute peace. We made mistakes, from habit more than intentions. Danced with our demons and jumped into bad dreams. Talked, cried, opened each other's wounds and in the end learned to accept that we could love. That in the Us, there was joy and peace. And that we would help each other to cross seas and chose the most beautiful path. And now, there is just me, with your urn, your candle and a razor blade. I need air, need to move. Running, stumbling up the stairs, unsure where to go, unsure of anything but the big hole in the middle of me. The car takes me, I can hardly see the road, but I know where we need to go. The priory, tucked away from the road, invisible to most, at the edge of a small village. Rough stones, more an outline than a building. I sit in a corner of the long-deserted space with spectacular views over the Downs, where they grow surprisingly good grapes.

Maybe there has been music, once, a long time ago. No sign of the wood that must have created a ceiling. A great hall and I can imagine the vast fire blazing on one side of the room. Monks, resting, drinking, debating. Prayer, maybe. But maybe they went to the glorious church next to the hall to reflect. I used to pray, to have conversations with God. Argue, accept, plead and in the end abdicated thought. But the universe and I, we are not talking now. Maybe I am petulant, maybe he does no longer exist. Many years ago, I used to analyse God with my friends, who believed that God had died. But if something dies, it will have existed in the first place. My head can no longer grasp the concept of eternity or a being that is looking after me. Small things have become unsurmountable obstacles. Dusting your shoes, letting my hand rest on the urn every morning, making myself walk through a world that I can no longer understand or feel, daily tasks and conversations have become the big questions that make me wonder and ponder. I find a perfect alcove, whittled into the stone by time and the wind. Small and safe and just for you. I leave you amongst the ghosts of monks and their prayers. The ash crumbles under my fingers as I spread you into the small, hidden space. My hands are pale and lonely without your fingers resting on them. In the car, on our walks, when we sat and talked, your hands and mine were always linked. Every night, when I collected you, you asked about me and my day and my answer was always the same: Much better now. And we both knew this to be true. Unshakable truth that was Us. My hands are lonely without you. For a little while, I wander around the church and amongst the graves. Stones, some as old as the abbey, leaning towards the earth, as if they want to join those, whose names they bore, and which have long since been eroded. Would you have liked a grave; a stone to remind the world that you existed? You had asked to travel, not to have to stay in one place. But maybe, there was a small part inside you that would have liked your own special place. I wish I could build you a monument, make you immortal like the sea. Stone, houses, mountains, they in the end crumble under the wind and the rain. The sea takes, it never ends, cannot be eroded, eaten by some other part of nature. But how is it in my power to build a monument, an eternal memory of you? Arriving home, I glance at the candle in the window and wish for something other than this.

Two gnarled trees, twisting gently into each other behind a flint wall. Bathed in sun, but despite the warmth, somehow foreboding, two busts on either end of the wall. Gravestones of sorts, Virginia and Leonard Woolf, their ashes resting under the roots of the intertwining trees. The garden, large and beautiful with an endless view over the parched fields. Leona, my trusted friend and longstanding partner in crime, next to me, holds you in her hand. We brought you here to rest with two troubled souls in the garden they created to soothe their restlessness. Dragonflies hover over the water of a small pond, just behind us.

Your mother created a garden, her favourite lilac dominated the space, where she found some kind of peace. My children would never go into the garden we had when we moved to the coast. There were slow-worm and they thought them to be snakes. No amount of explanation would make them enter the large, rambling piece of land that I tried to tame.

 I remember their birth, vividly, clearly and sad. Two girls, born within a minute of each other, taken by gentle hands in a violent act, from my torn belly. Green cloth, splattered with blood hid the tiny beings from me. They were taken away in a matter of seconds. Taken to warming plexiglass cots far away from me. Machines monitoring, reporting, bleeping to keep them safe. And whilst the gentle hands sewed my torn skin, their father was able to follow the small cots and the entourage of green coated nurses and doctors. My empty belly no longer of interest. On the ward, with other mothers, who had babies, real babies, who cried and drank and slept, someone gave me a picture, two pictures of tiny creatures with woolly hats. The other babies had visitors, were cooed over and admired. I never really liked the look of new-borns. There were flowers from their new grandfather, their father's father. Proudly, he showed me that my children were the first twins in their long family tree since 1719. The last children to have the family name. He was not unhappy that they were girls. He had soothing words and left. And downstairs, where the small, the unformed, light ones, who needed extra care to life, their grandmother, with her cold catholic eyes, took possession, took charge. A Spanish Contessa no less. Once beautiful matriarch, she claimed her grandchildren for her clan. Like your children claimed you. She had waited patiently for this moment and would wait even more patiently to claim them completely. She and my children's father, sitting next to the clear cots, admiring and making plans amidst the white tiles and sterile bedding. You never met my children, not the twins, nor my son. What would you have thought of them? And in this beautiful garden, made by a strong, broken, wondering woman, I grieve for my children as well as you.

We shared dreams, long before we knew each other, of large tables and family. Of arguments and laughter, of a clan and love. Neither of us were able to shape our lives to create a reality. Our flaws were too large, too unforgivable to make our children want to remember us as we were. Your biggest fear was to be misunderstood, judged. Punished for being who I am, you used to say. As long as we could hold onto each other, we escaped punishment and would not stumble into the judgment of others. The judgment of those, whom, despite everything, we love most.

Leona, brightly coloured, dungaree clad; Leona, holds my hand and together we feed you into the foot of the wall, at a point between the two busts, in the shadow of the intertwined, loving trees. We walk amongst the sweet-smelling phlox. Bees and butterflies hurry through the flowers. We amble towards the small church next to the garden, where Virginia Woolf wrote. Cool, medieval air surrounds us as we admire stained glass windows and polished wood. I am sure that God, the Entity, the Universe lives amongst the flowers, the pond, the dragonflies and bees and does not hide behind these beautiful windows, depicting a virgin mother with a startlingly white infant, born amongst dark skinned people. Leona and I spend some more time at the wall that separates the graveyard from the writer's garden and the fields beyond. I leave a little of you here, my Darling, just for the view. And in the soft heat of the day, it feels as if we have found a perfect place for you to marvel over the seasons and the endless sky.

Travelling with your Ashes

Unspeakably tired; just breathing and walking has become exhausting. I am not sure my Darling, for how much longer I can drag this body around and make it appear to be functioning. I am teaching a little, working most evenings, running youth clubs and hope that nobody will discover that all I can really hear is your last breath. How much of the world can I make yours when I struggle to stay upright and when it takes all of my energy not to crumble and howl? I have lost all interest in our cave. I dust when I have to, hardly ever change the bedding. Pick up your things and place them carefully back where they were. Without you, it makes as little sense as me.

I attend meetings, respond to letters and emails. I still refuse to wear uniforms and struggle with misplaced authority. I have to attend another meeting, away from the offices, on some farm in the middle of the countryside. There are piglets and goats, there are sheep and chickens. I remember the smell of hay, remember building houses out of straw and hiding from them in the late summer sun. My mother's people, people of the land, from a place endlessly flat and indifferent identity. The soil does not know if it is Danish or German and it does not care.

My people have hard hands, thick, sunburned necks and bright blue eyes under red hair. The sound of cows, with bursting udders waiting to be led into the warmth of the milking parlour soothed me into sleepiness. Collecting eggs in the first morning light, my aunt's frying pan sizzling over the fire, waiting for the eggs to arrive. Beacon from our pigs.

On pig slaughtering days, I always walked as far away as I could. Pigs have knowing eyes and shrill, frightened voices. Four farms and the big house, that is our place in the world; our genetic inheritance. My great-grandfather, who later hung in the apple tree, belonged to the people in the big house. A rich farmer, owning boundless acres of land and enough people to make him richer, the family still holding most of the fields, was my great-grandfather's master for many years. And after a while, a lifetime of labour he gave him land to build his own farm. The apple tree was already there and next to it, my great-grandfather built his house, substantial, with space for people and animals under one squat roof. He had four sturdy sons, shaped for work and born with the skin of farmers. But my grandfather, his youngest, who was meant to inherit what was now a flourishing holding, did not have much appetite for the land. He wanted to leave and started to work in a dairy, not far, but far enough so that he could no longer hear the cows and the chickens and feel the guilt of his desertion. Eventually he moved to what we considered the South, married my small, beautiful grandmother with her dancing mind and worked at the docks of Hamburg. And his next older brother took on the farm; the land parcelled up, to build two more farms of the same size for the others. Summers spent in the blazing heat, bringing in the harvest, skipping amongst my aunts neat rows of green beans and asparagus; jumping into cow pads with my cousins; winters when we had to stay inside and slept with the cows. The freedom of a landscape where nobody can disappear because the earth is flat and the horizon low. And just beyond the horizon was the sea, endless promise of a whole globe full of adventures. Small, proud me, skipping between cultures, languages, the big city and the place not large enough to even be a hamlet.

And now, I find myself again sitting amongst piglets, who are gently nipping my feet and exploring my skin, with their mother looking on. And, although I have the greatest respect for their teeth, however young they are, I stroke the skin between their eyes, until they fall to their sides. Comical little creatures, playing under the watchful eyes of their large mothers, looking for mud and pleased that their offspring are not trying to feed for a few minutes. My black dress, now covered in mud and straw, is no longer suitable for a serious meeting. I have left my shoes at the gate and as my face rests on one of the warm bodies, I can breathe the air of a past when everything seemed possible. I am part of the damp air, the wind, unchecked by trees or buildings. And I am part of the apple tree that still appears in my nightmares, with the dangling figure of a stiff, old man. When I finally make it into the meeting, I am late and cannot even fake interest. All I know that there is some sort of peace here. A peace I have not felt for a long time, not since the Sunday mornings before you left.

Travelling with your Ashes

My hands are still shaking sometimes. My fingers, flattering butterflies without purpose, trying hard to tie the ends of the balloon. Today, my Darling, you will fly; really fly. I stop and stare at the rings on my hand. Silver, our wedding bands, still welded together, the engagement ring we bought in the little coin shop nestles next to the small band of Celtic weave. You had one that matched but lost it and then insisted that we would buy another matching pair. I hold my face against the rings, trying to steady my fingers, cool my face on the narrow metal bands.

Was any of Us real? Or is it just your death that not based on dreams? Not a sanitised death, the ones you hear about from friends, over the phone, in a message. Our death, quietly, with my hands on your arm and your half open eye. Our emptiness in the early evening, the pointlessness of me without Us, hover as a gigantic, untameable shadow over me. What would you do now? You would drink, no doubt. But would you have broken into a million little shards of opaque glass, trying to negotiate their way through the darkness? I take you, in your silvery balloon across the road, towards the beach. The pebbles glisten in the late afternoon sun. As I pass the trees on the green, I have to smile for a second. These were our trees, bending away from the wind. Shaped into crooked skeletons by years of storms and salty rain, they were your destination, every time you came home. Our trees. The balloon rattles above my head. Helium filled rubber, shining, sparkling, holding the small grains of ash as they are dancing in tune with the wind.

Aly, waiting for me at the pier, has weeping eyes again. She cries for you, for me, for Us. Aly, our companion on car-boot, flea-market and charity-shop trips; my brash, hardheaded and soft-hearted friend stands on the pier, waiting for us. I remember the Sunday, the first Sunday after you had survived a week of itching ants under your skin, sweats and unreal voices and eventually made your way slowly along the lines of treasures for sale in a field. Holding onto me in fear of collapse. You faced that week, when you tried to shed one of the demons from your shoulders, like you faced your last weeks. Stubbornly clinging onto yourself and me. I pleaded with you to seek help. I dimly knew that there would be medical support that could ease the suffering. But, whilst I dried your face and held your hands through the screaming and scratching, you had to face your enemy on your own terms. Your pain, unfiltered and raw was difficult to witness. Later, after we knew that there was nothing to hope for but a peaceful end, you refused pain relief for a long time because you wanted to know where your enemy was. You should have taken a place in Walhalla, my brave soul, my emperor. Instead, your demons killed you, took you and left me with their shadows laughing through the windows.

Aly holds the balloon for a minute, and we wait for the moment when the sun begins to drown over the Arun. And then I let your go, on a gust of wind, floating slowly over the river towards the changing light on the other bank. You rise and rise until I can see the sun through the balloon, the universe, the eternal setting and awakening of Rah takes you into its arms. The rays expand through the walls of your travelling vessel and my eyes follow you until you disappear over the horizon or into the clouds.

Negotiating my way across shiny floors under bright lights, I concentrate on my next step and you. Some say, you are with me, somewhere, always watching. I am not so sure. But, you are in my small case, next to my toothbrush and some paperwork, nestled, waiting to be released. Do you enjoy our travels? Do they mean the same to you as they mean to me? My legs are weak, I talk to myself in my thoughts. After the security checks, I only have to navigate through the even shinier floors of the duty-free palace, and then I can sit for a while. At the end of the conveyor belt full of cases, a uniformed man asks me to step aside. Has he found you? I have all the paperwork handy. After our last journey, I assumed that I did not have to mention you. What would I not give to have you standing behind me. I fluster and bluster, feeling guilty, as I always do when I am in danger to clash with officialdom. And as always, I have simply missed something. I have two lighters in my bag. Not that I am entirely sure why two lighters can do more damage than one, but I apologise. I am asked to make a choice, which one to keep and which one to leave behind. Incapable to make decisions, whilst it is hard to stay on my feet, I just point one of the two offending items. I need air, need to sit somewhere, away from the noise, the sparkling floors and the relentless, cruel light. The uniformed man, confident in his environment that frightens and confuses me, has another question. Although he has detected nothing else illegal amongst my clothes, he would like to know more about the grainy substance in small bottles. I can only stare at him, searching in all corners of my brain for an answer that would explain, without being offensive, leading Us into trouble and avoid missing the plane. All I can do is, to blurt out the truth – My husband, the grainy substance is my husband. Cannot bring myself to call you my late husband. You are not late, you are gone. I am not your wife; I am your widow. The man softens, asks when you passed. You did not pass anything or anywhere, you died. Not quite a year ago, you just stopped breathing and grew cold. His face changes, grows sad and tired. I don't want him to be sad and explain about our travels. About your ashes in suitcases and bags because you cannot walk with me. My eyes sting and I cannot talk anymore. The man has big hands with dark hair on the middle finger. He hands me the lighter and as I look at him, I can see that he is crying. I am free to go, free to take you with me and show you more of the world. My stomach heaves and cramps. I make it to a bathroom and try not to draw any more attention to Us.

We arrive in Athens without any further problems. I leave the airport. Only my overnight bag, no need to wait or linger. Looking for Dimitris for safety. Dimitris, my Greek friend, musician, eternal pessimist, has agreed to meet me at the airport. Friends for 30 years, we shared music and laughter in the hidden basement pub. Small space, always overcrowded, always smoke filled. Posters and announcements overlapping each other on walls that might once have been white, or maybe yellow, now an early nicotine magnolia. Music and food for all until 23:00. Then music and ouzo for those who had finished work somewhere else and stumbled down the stairs into the warm air. Ahmed, who could extinguish candles with a swish of his hand. Algerian, king of the kitchen who made couscous for those who came after midnight. Thin and ouzo filled, he danced whilst cleaning the kitchen and searched for people to argue with. And we sang, we danced and cried over nothing in particular. People of the night, finding warmth and friendship in what was, after all, the oldest music pub in our city. Named after the greatest Greek musician, who according to legend had once been a visitor in the low-ceilinged cave. Years of twilight and music shared and remembered by those who have survived.

Dimitris, once a tall, lanky guitar player with a gravelly voice, long black locks and a great love for all things sweet, has for a long time offered to show me his city. Had I not seen him a few years ago, I would not have recognised him. The locks have gone, but the voice, the voice of a sad singer, has not changed. I cannot be sure, when he moved back home to Greece, but it must have been sometime after I left my city. No matter, I have arrived and in the car, we talk about the old days, people we miss and songs we still sing. I try to explain my mission, but somehow, he is distracted by rising inflation and cost of living. He has visited our city more recently than I have and grieves for all that is lost. The past is lost, indelibly erased. No more small venues and playing until the sun rises. He still sings and fills larger halls. He has a dog and a pension. Athens is cold, bitterly cold. There has been snow a few weeks back. And the Germans paid for the airport. We arrive at my Air-B-And-B. I retrieve the key and Dimitris sees me upstairs. He leaves with the promise of coffee tomorrow.

The apartment is cold, modern, with water stains on the ceiling. Two balconies. I smoke in the darkness and watch the traffic. One of the apartments opposite is lit and I can see books lining the walls, wish I could find out what they are and maybe discuss some with their owner. Trying to plan tomorrow, the madness of my mission suddenly weighs me down. A busy main road between me and our destination. Twenty years ago, I was gripped by a Greek condition, an affliction known even then. Agora, misleadingly seen as just a marketplace. The outside became a frightening place. Agora is a place in a city, where gatherings are held; a place for people. And I fought my way back, overcame the phobic part during the hardest battle I could deliver. But still, there are some remnants of these demons lingering on my shoulders.

Suddenly I am back in a light filled classroom. Greek phrases and long-lost words return. Not useful now, they belong to a different time, tell different stories. I preferred Greek to Latin. Better stories, less war and more bearded, naked men in barrels, spending their time thinking and debating. Found solace in Plato, when Caesar bored me. The Greeks and the Romans travelled differently and sought different treasures. But they all invaded our young minds with irregular verbs and declinations. Whilst Caesar tried to conquer my unyielding ancestors, the Greeks found comfort and time for discussion in warmer places. I used to love the Spartans. Where is Sparta now? I find a map and hope that I can take you there one day. There seems to be little left, but to walk on that earth and leave you in the shadow of olive trees, whose ancestors have seen the great warrior race, is still something you might value. My mind, full of you, full of fear of having to cross a main road and the hope that Dimitris might be our guide, cannot rest easily. I hold you in my clenched fist, suddenly angry and sad. You should be here, your body should be with me, and your eyes should be able to see whilst I tell you the stories of Plato and caves and young men, who kill their fathers or others, who drift through labyrinths. But like Icarus, you burned on your way to some other place.

There is no news from Dimitris. He is busy. How will I manage to take us to the Acropolis? The street outside the apartment is narrow and busy. Manageable. But at the end it flows into the bustling dual carriage way I will have to cross. It might as well be the Aegean Sea, waves clashing, making crossing impossible. I cannot swim that distance. The palms of my hands are wet; dizzy, disoriented, confused, my mind scrambles. You, in your glass bottle, burn in my hands. I have promised. We will go. I manage to find a way to call a taxi. The driver appears confused, murmuring something about a 10-minute walk. But he still accepts the fare and we arrive. You and I have arrived at the foot of the mound covered in small, slim trees and monuments. For a while, we sit amongst the trees. Ambling, clean paths lead towards the entrances. Benches line the walk. I squeeze you tightly. We have arrived and I will leave you amongst the Greek Gods. The sun, slowly breaking through the greyness of the morning begins to warm my back. No longer shaking, I make my way up through the trees and towards the ancient stones. Sanitised, clean, preserved. Glass railings lead up to the top of the mound.

People, an endless stream of people. Nobody alone. Taking pictures of each other, with each other. I hold you tighter. You are safe in the palm of my hands. I am your eyes, our eyes. Can you see? Can you imagine how the old Greeks worshiped Athena? How powerful they must have felt so high above the city.

Akron – high; I remember. The highest point of the ancient town. Despite the throng of people, there are quiet spaces. Spaces where we can sit and look over this vast sprawling monster of a city. I leave you in an excavation shaft and at one of the columns of the Pantheon. I hate leaving you behind. I watch the small patch of grey as it becomes part of the monuments and the landscape and smile. And I see me, lonely, black bird, lost without wings and cold in the feeble March sunshine. There is scaffolding around the Acropolis, and I am not surprised. Things need to be shored up, preserved, fixed. Nobody could fix Us. Unfixable, broken Us. I make my way back to the bottom of the gardens. Near me, a couple discusses the war in Europe. Fitting somehow. Why does the world not stop for you? Surely, there would have been a new silence in a world without you. The world should have gasped, sight deeply at an existence without you and a war in Europe. Your departures have not made any ripples in the flow of eternity and people discussing events in Ukraine as a hypothetical, not the dirty reality that it really is. I need to be alone, disappear.

On the wide avenue, full of vendors of all things tourist, I stop for a while in front the statue of Maria Callas. More beautiful in bronze than in life. You should have something that lasts forever, undying and seen, bearing your name.

You should have legends woven around you, grow immortal. For now, I have given you one of the largest gravestones, on the top of a mound full of Gods and Goddesses. Looking back at your resting place close to the sky, I wave, quietly, imperceptibly. These streets are designed for tourists, bustling, easy to navigate, but there are no interesting doors. I find a smaller shop, full of dust and cheap statues, probably made in China. I need to buy something to add to your things. The lady, tiny, dark and helpful, points at things. Lovely, glittering earrings, icons and the protecting eye. As she wraps my memories, she asks why I am here. Alone, business or pleasure? Women on their own are not the norm amongst the tourists. I explain. It has become easier to say that you and I are travelling together. I am not alone. You are in my pocket. And then I suddenly cry. Black, lost crow in a forgotten souvenir shop. The tiny woman holds my hand, sudden, warm, human. Another hand over mine. She smiles. She hopes I will come back and visit the city and have tea with her. We both know that I will not return, my mission in Athens has been completed, but her smile is comforting.

I have to find a way back to the apartment. Crossing the sea of cars, not stumbling, using my useless legs. I slow down, walk as deliberately as I can. Find smaller and smaller streets. Narrow streets full of beautiful doors and crumbling graffitied walls. Fewer people. The mound behind me; I have studied the way on the map. Sketched what might be manageable. I can see the first main road. Traffic lights. People crossing. Nobody stumbles. Normal people are surefooted and clearheaded. I take a deep breath and assemble your walking stick. Something to hold on to. Something to steady me. Something real in my hand to calm the demons in my head. You never used the stick, but we ordered it anyway, just in case, like so many other things that might have made things easier. My fingers tightly curl around the last little glass bottle and my other hand clings to the walking stick. I made it. Across the road, into a park. Parks are green, safe and I can breathe again.

I make my way along the road, past a stadium, watch a group of young people practicing their football skills. The pavement is uneven. The trick is too slow down my steps when all I want to do is run. Slow my steps and slow my heartbeat, remind myself that all of this is just a play my demons perform in my head. No tourists here. Broken walls and sickly trees. Some steps lead down to what appears to be another park. An oasis maybe? A place to settle my stomach and steady my legs. I find a church. It has a name, I like places with names. I always wanted to live in a house with a name; lived in two and was unhappy. Maybe I should avoid houses with names, however beautiful they are. The deserted, insignificant church with locked doors and cats strolling over the small square in front has a name. Agia Fotini Ilissos, dappled sunshine covers the cobbled square, a small shrine in one corner, flanked by Greek flags. The air feels soft after the rain and for the first time there is something like spring filtering through the clouds. One of the cats strolls over. Grey and white, wide eyes with a thin tail. We stare at each other for a while, but decide against further contact. This is the place you would love. Not the Acropolis, the gardens and statues. We should go to Sparta, my Darling. We will go. The cats are appearing from under bushes, trees the shade next to the church. Tails erect, they run towards an unseen visitor, follow a call or a timetable. From one of the hidden paths, a woman emerges. Plastic bags, talking softly to the cats, calls and coos. The cats rub along her legs, the plastic bags. They have expected her. She crosses the square and enters a small clearing in the undergrowth. Rustling bags and the clicking sound of tins being opened. More than ever I feel like an intruder in a world where things have purpose and timings. She re-emerges, visible moved, unsettled, calling. The same word, a little louder every time. It might be a name. Her voice is hoarse and deeper than I had expected. She rushes along the edges of the square, around the church, into the undergrowth and amongst the spindly bushes. She returns, upset, lost. A wave of unknown words hits me, urgently and frightened. I don't understand her, and she does not understand me. And yet, it becomes clear that one of her homeless charges is missing. We call and search together for a while, until she shrugs her shoulders, wipes her face, smiles at me with a thin, rainy bending of her lips and returns to the rest of her family, collecting bowls, whispering words and then leaves.

This is a good place for us. I can leave you here, amongst the cats and watched over by a saint and a lady, who cries over a missing stray. Next to the grey, yellow stones, a small, crippled tree is searching for light and survival. I open the last of my little bottles and set you free under this tree. This is a good place for you. A place, I will remember and might even smile at the memory. For now, I am making my way back to the apartment, not caring anymore if I stumble. Tomorrow I will spend some time at the museum, a glass and concrete colossus, designed to imprison statues and Gods in white light and sterile safety. Preserved, chained, captured, bereft of context and meaning. Designed and constructed by architects, separating art from life. A difficult relationship full of tension between the past and future, manifested in this cold place. I will have coffee on the terrace and write some poems under your watchful eye from your place at the Acropolis whilst listening to foreign voices and words. And then my Darling, I will have no reason to return. I know where you are, and I know that you are in the place under the spindly tree fighting for life.

In the taxi to the airport, I watch the sprawling, all-encompassing city disappearing behind the mountains and wonder about friendship, time and the fruitlessness of either. Maybe I was meant to wander around Athens on my own, see myself in the harsh light of reality. Lonely, lost woman, overtaken by time, growing old without noticing and lonely without expecting it. Maybe one day Dimitris will explain his absence, and it will not matter. I turn my face towards the window and the mountains to avoid the driver seeing my tears.

You hated birthdays, generally struggled with celebrations and occasions. Unsure how to react to kindness, you could become cold and detached. You craved and loathed attention in equal measure. You disliked cake and did not know how to respond to presents. So, I made a cake for you and we fed it to the birds, left the presents next to your bed whilst making our morning coffee. No wishes over candles or bad, but enthusiastic singing. Last year, I bought you the best bottle of rum I could find, and we played chess in the early morning, whilst the seagulls fought over the cake and the cream. I don't have the strength to bake, have not used the cooker since you left. But I bought a present for you. Two sepia-coloured pictures of Greek lovers. Peaceful, remote faces, leaning into each other at rest and trust. They are yours, my Darling, and I hope they speak to you in some way.

I filled a little of you into small rubber ducks. Colourful children's toys, designed to float on the water, with enough space to accommodate you. And I know the place, where I will set them free onto the tide. The beach, we both loved because it is devoid of people and shops. No arcades and swirling sings, no fish and chips and sticky ice-cream. Just the shore and the waves. The storms have taken most of the beach away, crushed the defences and felt the few trees that were standing guard. The water came inland and flooded the land, leaving it salty, silty and barren. Concrete boulders litter this small part of the coast; unordered, chaotic as if thrown from the skies by some angry, uncontrollable God. Small birds with black heads and long, spindly legs run along the sand, avoiding the waves whilst keeping their eye on the prey they might miss. I leave my shows on one of the boulders and my feet feel their way across the pebbles and the bright green moss that seems grossly unreal in the apocalyptic landscape. Do you remember the day, when we walked along this beach, under this sky; when I showed you the tree of my soul, grown from concrete, roots cast in stone and yet somehow able to live. And when the storms came and carried the barriers and walls away, they left those roots exposed to the light. The tree a silhouette against the stark sky, cut in half and yet clinging on to something invisible that did not allow it to die. And we sat, with the barren fields in our backs, facing the unending waves clashing against the land.

I find a small cove, where the pebbles shine clear and clean through the water and in the dying sun, I set 6 tiny rubber ducks swim away from me. One for every decade that this world should have known, loved and cherished you; and a small bottle with you and some feathers for the future you did not have.

The roofs of Albania greet me like an old friend. Weathered terracotta tiles, many no longer forming a coherent whole, bask in the autumn sunshine. The buildings seem to sink into the soil, seeking shelter and over time will disappear from view. Albania's people abandon houses and farms, they just leave one day and never return. They leave furniture, clothing and their parents to search for a future under a different sky, where the roofs are not claimed by the earth and the winds. I want to wrap my arms around these old houses, full of history and tears. Want to share my screams with them, nest in the dark and amongst the brambles penetrating the decaying window frames. Lean my face against the doors and whisper stories into the wood.

Far away from the marble cathedrals of tourism, due south from Durres the country is dry and hot. Fier, small and dusty hometown of Ledja's parents reminds me of journeys taken when I was not much more than a girl, exploring the world, which seemed to be endless and full of wonders. Journeys through the Turkish mountains and small Iranian towns. Ledja's grandfather, observing the world through sparkling eyes of undefined colour greets us with a schoolboy grin that covers the whole of his round face. His wife, even smaller than her husband, bustles and smiles, although nobody seems to know where her mind is at any given moment. Finally, she sits next to me and holds my hand. We drink coffee and some strange home-made raki on the wide terrace, shaded by vines bearing large green grapes. A young man, who speaks some English translates my questions. The old man's face twinkles when he talks about the time under the communists, the bunkers and the villages. Once, everyone was a communist, and living was dangerous. I learn the word for prison – burgu. He was never in prison but explains how easy it was to fall foul of the system, to be arrested and just disappear. When the young man asks him if he still feels like a communist, he does not answer, but his eyes shine brighter. We laugh and Ledja's mother explains my story to her parents. The old woman holds my hand even tighter and leans her head against my shoulder. She is so small, that her head fits nearly into the crook of my neck.

What would they make of you? Of your colour, your beautiful soft eyes? What would you make of them? Suddenly I know that you would have discussed grapes, climate and wine with the old man and that you would have enjoyed the home-made clear spirit served in small glasses. Humanity shared over food and drink and the language of gestures. I want to take your hand and sit with you on this terrace. I want to close my eyes and let the strange language over me, with my skin drinking the sun and the warmth of these people.

Paradise nestles just outside of Fier. Apollonia, the most beautiful of all your resting places. The most confusing, most important and most fitting place to leave you lies in the most unexpected piece of land. Few tourists and the only person who appears to be looking after this site is the man at the gate who collects a laughably low entrance fee. We wander amongst ancient olive trees and seemingly randomly placed stones. And suddenly, there is a Corinthian façade. Columns supporting a structure long since abandoned. All that is left are the columns, some steps and the pediment. We walk along a small path of Roman paving, which suddenly ends on the side of the hill, overlooking the valley beyond, littered with Igloo shaped bunkers of various sizes. The crazy legacy of a paranoid dictator. A tortoise saunters from the undergrowth towards my feet. I sit in the hot dust and watch the ancient creature making its way towards a fresher, more inviting plot of grass. Slowly, deliberately, it moves leg after leg, ungainly and majestic. It makes me laugh, its determined, ungainly movements produce an unexpected speed. I am a tortoise in many ways. Seemingly indestructible, moving slowly, determinedly towards an uncertain future. With skin that seems to be thick and impenetrable, but that is in reality soft and vulnerable and will retract into the shelter of its armour as soon as pain threatens to open old wounds. And when some disaster that cannot be avoided, turns the lonely creature to lie on its back, it is nearly impossible to right itself again. The tortoise disappears into the long grass on the other side of the path and I hope it finds a rich grazing ground. Sitting on one of the rocks, overlooking the valley and the Illyrian burial mound, I feel overwhelmed by all this visible past surrounding me. You will love this view and resting with bronze age people. So many feet have crossed these paths, breathed this air and many are buried here.

A familiar sound brings me back to this day, this present, this now. Sheep. A shepherd begins the climb along the mound. His sheep are smaller, longer legged than mine at home. Amongst them a goat, young and lost, but following the tribe it somehow has strayed into. The man, tall, with dark skin, follows the animals, who do not require his presence as they are protected by his dog. The dog wanders seemingly aimlessly amongst the grey and white animals, but I am sure that his small eyes are trained on every single one of his charges. I want to ask the man about grazing and the breed of his sheep, but I very much doubt that we share a language.

James and I carry on with our climb up the mound, following the sheep, whilst the shepherd rests at the half-way point. On the other side, where the terrain is flat and the grass filled with wildflowers, we find some steps and an entrance into the underground world of the communists. We follow the steps and the tunnel they lead into. Another leftover from the dark times in Albania. Tunnels, endless tunnels, filled with rubbish and graffiti snake their way along the sides of the mound. Every so often, there is a set of steps leading to the bright outside of the meadow, with another, identical set opposite opening the way into another tunnel. They smell musty and damp and after navigating my way through six of these bizarre constructions, I am glad to be back in the hot sunshine and under the sky. On our descent, we meet the shepherd, who is still resting. The sheep can be heard in the distance, and I convince James to try his language skills to translate my questions. The man, suspicious at first, stares at my face and then talks about his sheep and life in the open. James warms to the idea to find out more about the thoughts of this weathered man with the dark skin and the brown eyes, deep set under heavy brows. He is a Vlach or Aromanian, from a wandering people, who keep sheep and goats and don't adhere to borders. He believes in capitalism and is completely at ease with his herd, grazing amongst ancient burial places and monuments. They plug greenery wherever they find it and are unconcerned with history and the gravitas of centuries. We watch them climbing the steps of the amphitheatre, or what is left of it and take our leave.

This place has been loved by the bronze and iron age people of the Balkans, the Greeks, Corinthians and Romans and later by the communists. We explore the ruins of storage caves and something that might have been a theatre or a debating site. For a long time, this place had been famous for education, learning and sophistication. And leaving the Romans and Greeks behind, we walk through another olive grove towards the Byzantine monastery, with its dark, beautiful chapel and covered walkways full of ancient statues. The cool air in the church and the courtyard is surprising and welcome. And then I face her – a statue of extraordinary beauty.

She is probably Greek, her stone skin somehow translucent and velvety. Her face is perfect and sad. I nestle next to her and touch her face, trying to dry my tears by stroking her cheeks. And then I leave a little of you at her feet. All that I had so fruitlessly looked for in Athens, I find here. Perfect statues amongst crumbling stone and sheep grazing amongst the bones of ancient people. I light a candle in the small church, amongst the gilded icons and dark, damp wood. The floor, uneven and chipped, still colourful in places, is covered in wax marks around the two sand-filled candle troughs. James and I sit for a while on the stone steps leading up to more covered walkways. We talk about you and the hole in the middle of me, our travels and the importance of my journey with you. About this strange paradise, full of ghosts, but grazed by sheep, goats and tortoises. As I look back over the site, I am glad that you are here, and I know I will visit you again. In this place inhabited by emperors, scholars and peasants, all of you, every single part of the kaleidoscope that is you; you can play the joker, the king and most of all, be the only person who could share my soul.

I have never slept well or long, but now it feels as if I do not sleep at all anymore. I need you with me, next to me. Your angel sister assures me time and time again that you are with me. Others talk of feathers or birds as messengers send by you. If I could just believe them, maybe things would be easier. But I cannot believe in feathers or signs, ghosts and probably not even in the Universe. I am lacking faith, vision, hope. Having tried their pills, talking, resting, working, reckless one-night-stands, painting, writing, drink, clairvoyants and meditation, I cannot escape the deep, dark void. It has become the sum of all pain, all scars, all losses and dead dreams. And the darkness grows. Every day, it is a little bigger and a little less visible to others. Two lives in one body. My soul has escaped with you and yet, I am still here. What is left of me is still here and does whatever seems to be required to survive. On some days, I wish I had never met you, had carried on, lonely amongst people in my perfectly acceptable world full of noise and distraction.

There has been too much death in the last few years. Too many memories, now just held by me. Me, the last keeper of moments committed to memory. No longer shared past. Just mine now. A year before I met you, I travelled home. I don't often visit the city of my youth, and never the countryside full of memories and cousins. My children did not want to travel, explore, learn my language or the bizarre mix of cultures of their mother.

A weekend to celebrate the years spent in our basement pub that has disappeared as most things inevitably do. All of us, who are were still here, coming together, making music, drinking Ouzo, musing over those who have been lost to the years and yellow pictures of our younger selves, who believed in a never-ending world and our ability to build utopia. A weekend to breathe the clear, rough sea air and visit another ghost from my past. Guenter, small, hungry looking revolutionary who tried hard to grow a beard, but who never managed more than a few wispy strands on his chin. Our small flat at the top of a four-storey building had been constructed after the war as emergency accommodation for those who no longer had a home. Two rooms under the roof, the corridor shared with the other tenants, who had their attic spaces up there, stored their coal and winter coats next to our kitchen where my lipstick melted in the summer. He, a mature history student and me, a small schoolgirl, who had escaped shadows and demons. Our rooms were forever cold in the winter and tropical in the summer; there was no warm water or a shower. And yet, we had morning light, music, books and dreams. I learned chess and painted one room, the one with the two-ring cooker next to the sink that balanced on one leg and a pile of newspaper, in a shrill blue, because the paint had been cheap. Both of us worked at night in the pubs and then attended lectures and lessons during the day. Suddenly, my Latin made sense. Helping him with research on medieval popes, this dead language of Caesar's war accounts became a living thing that I could understand and that had a purpose other than passing exams.

On Fridays we stood at the mouth of the motorway and hoped our thumbs would take us quickly to his parent's village, where we would have warm food, a bath and meet friends. We hitched lifts across Europe, made it all the way to Ireland. We took our leaking tent to every demonstration we could reach. The air was full of future and convictions, of righteousness and the arrogance of youth. At 14 I was a survivor, worker, student, no longer a daughter and the shaper of my own path. And then there came the child that I did not have. Nestled in one of the tubes, lost on its way. Many poems for that child are still caged in small black books with red spines, somewhere on my shelves. The doctor was sympathetic and efficient, could not stop the loss of the ovary. I had not wanted a child, not then, but when the large man in the white coat, accompanied by an equally tall nurse spelled out the facts, unavoidable and final, that I might never have children, my whole being span on its axis and became desperate. He was wrong, of course, and in the end, I greeted my son in the same hospital seven years later. I left the gentian-blue room, the attic and the medieval popes. Could not stand still, sit, rest, became part of the wind and refused to grow roots. Nobody's fault, no blame, no bitterness, just paving new paths with old tears.

Years later, we found each other again, friends who had shared part of a journey once. Messages about life, books we read and memories of shared travels. Many years, more than thirty had not given us wisdom, but distance and acceptance of the youths we once were. We could laugh at our dreams, at the uncouth believes in our immortality and strength. On this weekend, I visited Guenter. He had inherited his parent's house. I did not recognise much of it, apart from the garden and the front door. He had married and lost his wife. Snoopy, my faithful, long-suffering friend drove us to the village, listening to my musings, my fear to meet my past. Guenter, now riddled by cancer, had asked for a game of chess with his wilful student from so long ago. Had it not been for his voice, I would not have recognised him. Years and medication, designed to heal, had changed him from a skinny young man with freckles, long hair and a wispy chin into a big, clumsy body, who only retained his voice and his dancing eyes. His path had been painful, but straight; he had stayed, never became a historian, never discovered hidden treasures. But there was not regret, no wondering about the wonders he had never seen. A contented life without big mountains or valleys. We talked. Snoopy and I had planned to stay for an hour but talked for three. We never played our last game of chess. We talked about our travels, activism, marriages and deaths. He reminded me of struggles with my mother, tears and the baby as well as the butterflies I cried over at the roadside and our disastrous journey to Ireland that had cost him two front-teeth. We talked about tinned ravioli and strong French cigarettes we bought from the Corse in the pub at the corner. And when we left, I promised to return in a few months, before Christmas, absolutely before Christmas. Why do we always mark the year and our plans around Christmas or Easter? When we left, I felt heavy with memories and old songs. I had not played chess for a long time. I never painted any room in such a violent colour again. And yet, that time, like so many other times are part of me.

Guenter died a week later. He had been prepared and was happy to join his wife. For most of my life, we had not been close, had not seen each other for many years, during which we did not miss each other and created our own stories. And yet, he was the only link to my memory, made some of my past real. With him, I lost 18 months of my journey, and they will now only exist in my mind. With you, I lost my future. Why are events, past, present and future connected with people, who invariable leave me? I did not cry for him, not then. I still believed that everything happens as and when it must and that would be an After.

And sometimes, grief is public and must not be disturbed. Dust of the past must not settle of the hymns of today. Loss on a stage that I refused to enter, for fear of opening old wounds or maybe just forgotten. Jan, friend of my youth, aspiring actor with a head full of dreams, son of a publican, who read poems in our pub, just before Christmas. My protector from fists and hider of my secrets; who drank with me on the doorsteps of Hamburg and sang for me under the statue of Bismark, whilst teaching me about theatre and submarines. Just after you and I built our nest in my cottage, he took his last breath and all I could do was to burrow myself into your chest and talk about the rain in my city and the port full of music and sadness. Quiet memories, just mine now. The loss of so many on my way; me still standing, walking and drowning in unshared recollections. And you kissed me, held me, whilst playing poker on your laptop. And that was enough, would have been enough forever to ease the heaviness of those shadows.

Will you ever become a shadow, a ghost from my past? Is there anyone, who can share memories of your youth with me? I need to understand the path you took that brought you to Us. The butterflies you cried over. I need to find a measure of the plans the Universe might have for me and to somehow accept the fact that I am still here, left behind, forgotten, cold and sleepless searching for you.

The leaves have not quite changed their colours yet, but the sun has become weaker and struggles through the morning mist. Leona, next to me, in sensible walking shoes, guides me through vineyards and across dark soil left after harvesting. My mind wanders, we should walk along this path towards the tree tunnel and ultimately the windmill crowning the mound ahead. Time and time again I had planned for us to visit this place of changing colours and drink in the view over the expanse of coast. But somehow, we had never quite made it. Spending Sundays chasing treasure or debating the world. Would we have ever walked this path? Would we ever have touched the trees forming the tunnel of leaves? In the end, you were not a natural explorer, found reasons to postpone some travels that we could have made. If you were still here, would you have really beaten your demons forever? Or would you have faltered, stumbled and lost your fight? Would we have lost Us amongst the waves of amber liquid and strange phantasies? On dark days, and today is one of them, I fear that we had just lived and illusion and that ultimately, you might have returned to what you knew, however much pain it caused you. Returned to hoop earrings and the people, who inhabit a different universe from anything I can understand. Leona assures me, tries to bring back the certainty of your love, of Us. We pick grapes, not quite ripe, but holding the promise of sweetness and full of sun. I leave a little of you amongst the exposed roots in the tree tunnel, wishing you could answer me, give me some certainty, some strength. As we make our way up the mound, we ponder over the nature of addicts, of their vulnerability and the strength needed to face the world. You were so strong, incredibly strong in some ways, and yet in others you were too weak to withstand even the softest breeze. Always avoiding the new, the unknown, and yet, embracing your last weeks with strength and stoic expectation. Running away, but returning, drawn back by invisible strings that you could not, would not sever. Overshadowed by women, shrugging away love and commitment, drowning your fear and your beautiful, wandering mind. Leona reminds me, as we sit in the damp grass surrounding the windmill, that you called me your queen, your life; that you wanted to end your commute to London, just to give us more time; that you gave me your demons to tame and looked for safety and future in Us. And I love you enough to embrace you in your entirety, the whole of you. Now, there is nothing to fill this empty space in me, you can no longer just hold me and disperse my fears. To laugh away my shadowy thoughts of you leaving me, in the end to return to the world you knew.

Leona helps my flattering fingers to uncork the small bottle and free you from the glass vessel, to leave you with this most beautiful of all views. She holds my shoulders, shaking collection of bones, racked with missing you and unable to find answers. Bad days come in many shades, there are those when I am overwhelmed with love and the enormity of having lost Us; and then are those like today, when I am unsure of the validity of our feelings and future; and on yet others, everything is overshadowed by the last imagine of you. You left me in darkness and only when I am looking for places to leave you, can beauty penetrate through the all engulfing black fog around me. Not good enough to keep you alive, to keep you with me; too weak to remain uncrumpled and upright. Not small enough to shrink into the earth, away from concerned eyes and old ghosts. Not alive enough to envisage a future, and not dead enough to avoid feeling the crippling cold under my skin.

We make our way back to the car and I retreat into our cave, holding the sleeve of your jacket against the skin of my face. Maybe love, like most other things that can tear us apart, torment and keep us, is just an illusion, a dream that can be cancelled out with time and dulled hope.

Kruja, high up in the Albanian mountains, used to be the capital of Albania once, when the Illyrians settled here. All Albanian children have to visit the fortress, now a shrine to Skanderbeg. His prominent profile, dominated by a large, hook nose and an even larger beard, pointing bravely forward, is the main feature on numerous mugs, towels and little cheap busts populating the mock bazar in the shadow of the castle. Newly laid cobbled stones run amongst two rows of small shops, and we have to avoid being manhandled into them by the shopkeepers, who stand outside the doors lying in wait for unsuspecting ramblers in need of trinkets to spark their memories. The sky looks dark and menacing as we make our way up the steep path to the castle. More shops, more shopkeepers calling, promising the cheapest silver, busts or carpets in the whole of Albania. With a start I realise, that this is the first time in this wonderfully confused country that I experience the onslaught of wares produced for tourists, who are to be coerced into the shops and are held captive by smiles and offers of tea and bargains until they finally melt and buy some memento that they might lose on the way home. I smile a little and wonder what you would make of this. And of course, I buy one of the little busts to be framed with other mementos of our travels.

Whilst the sky is growing increasingly darker, we reach the castle and talk for a while to a solitary gardener, who explains at length that he volunteers and is unpaid. We move on, more cobblestones lead to the entrance of the castle and the ruin of a tower behind it. The stones appear polished and shimmer in the half-light. And I breathe. There are sheep grazing on the steep slopes around the ruin. This is the perfect place for you to be. You now have your own castle, the home of a hero, who managed to unseat and dislodge the Ottomans and whose helmet somehow made its way to a museum in Vienna. Skanderbeg, unsure of his beliefs and teetering between religions became something of the father of Albania.

High in the Mountains, above the usual collection of beautiful roofs, surrounded by sheep, you can reign forever. My emperor, I found a seat for you under the sky, overlooking your kingdom, as confusing, contradictory and beautiful as you. James and I sit for a while, watching the changes in the sky and decide to visit the museum in the castle. Build to impress, to convey power and pride, it is sturdy and cold. For the first time, I see furniture that seems to speak of tradition and art. When we leave, we realise that we have escaped a heavy shower. The ground is wet and slippery, but the sun has returned and will dry the earth quickly. We pass one of the oldest olive trees in Albania and sneak swiftly past the unpaid gardener before he makes good on his promise to show us his house and feed us lunch. On our stroll through the village, we stumble across a small restaurant, hovering precariously over the mountain edge. We are waved into the kitchen to choose food and sit on the balcony, high above the roofs and next to a nest of swallows, who are busy repairing their home. And the pain, the overwhelming, unbearable pain is back. With all its might it has returned, churning my stomach and making me hold my breath. You should be here, at this moment, with James, you should be here and feel the soft mountain air on your face. Your eyes should follow my hand pointing at roofs and trees. You and James should make fun of me and my little dances when I find sheep and interesting doors. You should drink in this view, hold my hand and dream of a house in the mountains. My head spins and we leave. On the way back to the ocean, I cannot find words, just stare at the trees and cry a little. James is silent and I know that he is missing you, too. We arrive back in Durres and spend time with the children. We climb olive trees and eat ice-cream and somehow life is overtaking death. Your ghost is lost amongst the girl's laughter and demands for more ice-cream, cheap toys and snacks. My beautiful, spoiled goddaughter, reminiscent of a wild Frida Kahlo, breathes life into the empty space in me. She is the same age as my eldest grandchild. A sturdy, red haired boy with freckles and the neck of my farming ancestors. I have only seen him four times and his younger sister even less. But, as I am not the mother my children needed and wanted, I cannot the be the grandmother I so long to be. I would love to make rainbows in back-gardens for them, as I did for my children, chase sunsets and tell stories, sing silly songs and admire their sense of adventure in a world that is too big to explore in one day. I would love to help them discover and stumble across new moments of happiness. But I failed at being a mother, as I failed to keep you alive. Perla, this beautiful, dark eyed and wild haired being, wo tries to teach me her language and to convince me that she needs a new phone, holds onto my hand and we skip back to the ice-cream shop. ～～

The mornings are the hardest part of the day. Waking up without you, after a little disrupted sleep, you are still not there. Alone, I stare at the tree at the bottom of the bed. I have added another tree next to it, gnarled, naked, arms outstretched into the yellow of a leaden sky. Sometimes I am frantically trying to see what you saw. On your last day, you talked of livers amongst the branches. I still cannot see them, can only see the sadness of my friend, the painter, who paints his pain when he is tired from screaming at the voices in his head. The palms of my hands are still raw from my clawing nails, I am restless, I need someone to scoop me up, hold me, keep me warm; I need some time on a terrace in the late sunshine, with a blanked on my knees and a sunset to cry over. For the first time in an eternity, I want someone to look after me, care, take the boulders from my shoulders, so that I can just be. I need the world to stop, the real world to pause until I have found my breath or a way to join you.

I have learned to exist on my own, following my own rules, because I struggle with those that seem to apply to the world. Even when amongst people, I need to know how to escape, how to be safe. I can smell the brittle, dark green linoleum covering the stairs in the home of my childhood. Four floors, each containing two flats, connected by green runways that had to be polished every Friday. The sound of my father's footsteps acceding the stairs made my stomach churn and is still part of my nightmares. The smell of the polish, unwaveringly applied by my mother, often with my help, lives on in my nostrils and my memory. Our neighbours were a friendly couple, who owned a small, dusty-smelling hardware shop a little way down the road, next to the police station and a haberdashery. I always loved the smell of freshly cut wood and new nails. Mysterious drawers full of screws in all sizes, sandpaper by the meter and soft paintbrushes. Our neighbours, helpful, decent people, wore brown overcoats and smiled when they met us on the stairs. They were safe and reliable, older than my parents, they were quiet, not disturbing anyone and going about their days in the unnoticeable way those at peace with life have.

On the day when my nose was broken for the first time, and all I could see was the blood, rising into my eyes, with my head bending in strange directions, I felt no pain. I could taste the blood, could see nothing but bubbling red that seemed to have a life of its own, and I knew I that nothing would stop the blows hurling at my head. Up to this day, it had been my legs or my back, never my face. I could hear my mother screaming, the sound drowning amongst the thumps. And I escaped, slipped away, using the whole of my small body to push through whatever was in my way, ran towards the staircase and hammered at our neighbour's door. I clung to the wood keeping me from safety, hoping that someone might find me. I knew they were at home. It was a Sunday and the lights in their hallway promised rescue. I kicked at the door, used my fists to make them hear me, open the door wash my face. But as most friendly, quiet people, they did not open the door, waited until I was returned, dragged by my hair, back into the hell behind white curtains and silence. And the next time, I polished the green stairs, I knew that there would be nobody, nothing, that would safe me. And yet, one day, many, many years later, you did. You could not undo what is engraved on my skin, but I felt safe, did not need my turtle shell to protect me and showed you the vulnerable back of my neck in trust and love. I told you and your demons most of the things I had never found the words to tell anyone. You never interrupted and your demons and mine mingled and danced on the fire of untouched memories.

I fill two balloons with a little of you and helium. I need you to fly away, be free and take my secrets with you. Where will you travel? Where will you go? Will you join a flock of birds and fly to a warmer, happier place? Will you rest on a cloud until sheds its load and then come back to earth with the rain? I meet Leona at the beach, we will let you go after a hot drink. Sitting on the pebbles in the midday wind, we talk about you. If I talk about you, you will not, cannot die. We laugh at your antics and talk about struggles with drink and loneliness. I tie the two balloons to a stick, crusted with salt, a traveller from some unknown place who might guide you. And the three of us make our way to the pier, jotting out into the sea, flanked by the river on one side and the ocean on the other. You flatter in the wind, as if you are impatient to begin your journey without me. At the side of the river, we find a quiet place, where we will not draw too much attention and let you go. I wave at you, expecting you to rise towards the sun as you have done before. But the stick might be weighing you down, or you might not be ready to go after all and your balloons sink onto the river. Two dancing silver spheres amongst the tide and the fishing boats. You are drifting towards the marina and the red bridge, inland. We are following you to the first small curve in the river when the tide turns, and you are swept up by some dirty yellow foam, drifting back towards the sea. We are following you again, now towards the mouth of the river. You dance amongst the foam, reaching for clearer water, breaking free, but are caught by a branch. Leona and I follow you, urging you on, two middle aged women shouting at balloons, unable to leave until you have started your journey into the open waters. Others join us, staring at the water, not quite making sense of what appears to be some crazy experiment without clear purpose. We have longs since lost track of time and the midday sunshine has given way to a late afternoon haze. You and your balloons have drifted closer to the pier and the vast expanse of open water. We shiver and hope that your journey will be clear from now one. But, of course, the tide, that has allowed you to swim towards the sea has taken the water faster than you and your twirls and twists. The slimy posts of the pier jutting out a little into the river, covered in green algae that in a few hours will be covered up by the incoming tide, hold your progress, as you are stopped by the unyielding wood. Leona and I stare in disbelief, agreeing that this you playing the joker, making fun of my poetic dream of you sailing into the sea; the sun is beginning to set, whilst we are willing you on. Suddenly, one of the balloons breaks away from the stick and disappears. We ponder, where it possibly could have gone, whilst the other still rides on the waves, swaying in and out of the gaps between the groins. We stand in the fading light, drawn, captured by your journey, which somehow reflects the stream of your life. In the last light, like a small, scurrying animal, the last balloon shivers and disappears under the pier. You might rest there for the night or forever and somehow, we feel cheated and sad for you. You have not floated into the freedom I wanted for you, but buried yourself under the pier, where we sat in the summer, eating ice-cream and planning a future that never came. The crowd, we had attracted for a while, has long gone and I return back into our cave, to the trees at the foot of the bed, alone. Stroking the lid of your urn, I wonder what you would make of my hapless attempts to fulfil my promise. And suddenly, the smell of green linoleum invades my senses and I have to retreat into my armour, where I can protect your memory and my dying dreams.

Travelling with your Ashes

Fog engulfs the gentle hill in front of me. Walking next to Gabriel, I try not to slip on the autumnal mud under my feet. My fingers hold onto you in your glass bottle, secure and warm in my pocket. Gabriel, wise, sad searcher for truth ponders over my questions. We slowly climb towards Chanctonbury Ring; made for fog and slow sunrises. Pagans, Iron Age people, the Romans and apparently the devil found shelter and purpose in this mystical place. The trees, their bare arms stretching high into the milky mist promise to hold secrets and stay here forever. Maybe you are part of these trees, and all trees everywhere. Maybe you are part of this fog, this hidden sky and the mud under my feet. I am beginning to understand why some Buddhists sweep the path they are walking on, petrified that they might step on something that is really someone's soul. I you are part of everything, you should be part of me. I wish, not for the first time, that I could draw and paint, capture magic and make moments eternal. Trap birds and the wind, waves and berries. As we walk, we talk about ancient wisdom and truth hidden in all of us. I am taken back to many of our conversations, during the pandemic, in my tiny cottage. You believed in the devil and demons, in darkness and winding rabbit hole paths. I believed in light and understanding, in feeling and searching for truth and love. And so we forged Us. Your demons became softer, tamer, easier for you to carry. We researched the Sumerians and First Nation beliefs, ancient paintings and speculated over the purpose of structures that appear to grow from the landscape. The earth and the sky, the sea and the stones, eternal witnesses of humanity, worshipped and feared in equal measure. A tree, apparently dead, lying on its side, sinking into the earth, shows the first shoots from its base, creating another tree, or is reborn. A child or an eternal self. The trunk, resting and decaying, plays host and nursery to colourful moss and new branches. And underneath the wooden cover, larva stays warm and protected. In the small garden of my cottage, I found a pile of wood, created over years. Trees felled to make space for flowers or ponds, breaking into brittle parts and when I moved one of the logs, I found a nursery of stag beetles. I replaced the wood and waited breathlessly and impatiently for the majestic creatures to begin their flight into the summer sun.

The cottage was my place, my home, perpetually interrupted and disturbed by Jon and his mother. My displaced, lost friend, who could not fit into any world, neither the one he came from, nor the one he tried to create. First son of hard-working, unbending parents. His mother wrestled with his tantrums and nightmares, whilst his father took refuge in the pub. An unsuitable prince and heir for the empire build by two generations before him. A restless spirit, driven by hate and loneliness, he rebelled bitterly to find their love, or any love at all. His younger brother, practical, uninspiring and reliable became the prince, the heir, the pride of their parents, whilst Jon fled and travelled. They kept him in money and kept him away, build an empire based on geraniums and cacti. His rages hidden on the other side of the sea, whilst they found some peace in the ordinary. In Thailand, he finally found a place where people admired him, the European who brought rice for the village and build a house for a family. Toy, my lovely friend, Jon's partner of 12 years, with her long glossy hair and thin arms, liked to drink, or maybe, like you, she needed to numb herself to face the days, endless weeks and years ahead. Toy, who loved to dance and wear crazy wigs, whom Jon called his monkey, understood far more than her face would ever betray. During her visits, she would fry small fish in my kitchen and shriek at my apparently dangerous way of peeling potatoes. We would sit on the damp earth in the garden, eat the fish and silently agree on the impossibility of life whilst the others produced big plumes of grey, vile smelling smoke and talked about past adventures and glories that could not be verified.

And one night, in her village in Thailand, after having played cards with her cousins and staring at an empty bottle of scotch, Toy fell to the floor and did not wake up again. The call came at midnight and Jon's small world crashed into unbearable bleakness. He gave the house in the village away, along with Toy's pink bike and her pick-up truck. Jon never returned to Thailand, or indeed travelled at all. His tantrums and temper grew worse and with his intolerable loneliness, his sense of entitlement became unbearable. With my arrival at the cottage, I entered a universe of servitude, trapped in a small world with Jon and his mother. Both, each in their own way able to make me believe that they were doing much for me, whilst I painted the stables and cut the hedges; bringing the outside world with me when I came home, eagerly awaited by two lonely souls.

And then you, my Emperor, came into my world and my cottage. Unsettling a balance of dancers, the universe you and I built, collided with Jon, his mother and my business - partners. The stars realigned. You, tender and kind when you were the fourth at Sunday dinners, and the old lady, with so little apart from money, was glad when you and I cleaned the kitchen, whilst Jon glared at you from his seat at the table. The truce between you was uneasy and not destined to last. You held your tongue, Jon spat stories about his travels and smuggling diamonds.

And in the end, without any reason or event, we were asked to leave the cottage. I grieved and you packed my books into boxes. Too many boxes for one person's shelves. With confused stoicism, we gave up my small world and found our cave at the beach. The cottage, small, with the downstairs bathroom and steep stairs would not have been the right place for us to have those seven last weeks. I am glad that we lost the cottage and found the beach. Your last breath, in our bed, in our home, with the sound of the sea engulfing the room, was a good one, and I am grateful for that.

Just before we stacked the boxes and bags into the van to take us to our new life, Jon suffered a stroke during his sleep. He never woke up to see us gone, never had to suffer any more lonely days or break things to remind himself that he was alive. You took the news with a smile, I was sad. My head rested on your chest, and I prayed that nothing bad would happen to us. We had a lifetime ahead of us, whilst I could only hope that Toy and Jon would find each other again, in some place, closed to us. But Toy had believed in re-incarnation and they might miss each other on their new paths. Jon had built a shrine for Toy. In the corner of the room, he burned incense in front of the Buddha and a picture of Toy. I don't want to build a shrine for you. I want you to come home, to be with me, to let me rest my head on your shoulder. At times, when Jon could not drive, I took him to the Buddhist monastery. A place of utter peace and a strange air of acceptance. His friend, who changed his name into something I could not pronounce, a monk older than me, had woven his coffin and placed it above his bed. He was neither expectant nor frightened, simply had readied himself for whatever was to come at whatever point in the future. Re-birth, maybe there is such a thing for you, but I am not sure that you, the you I knew would have liked the idea. Would you repeat your mistakes, born from pain and an impossible deck of cards? Or would you allow your beautiful soul to shine in the shape of a worm or an eagle? I shake my head. Grapple with concepts of energy that remains, whatever we do or experience; with souls finding new avatars and children with old eyes. Somehow this seems to be as impossible as all other options; insufficient answers that leave me searching.

Gabriel and I have reached the highest point of the ring, surrounded by fog and trees, with a fine rain forming spider nets of droplets in my hair. He believes in re-birth, re-incarnation as well as becoming part of everything. He believes that tortured souls will return and return, until they can do good and finally rest. Placing some of you in the stone overlooking the valley, the air feels mystical, and the fog surrounds me, forms safe walls for us. I know that Jon was a tortured soul, but I wish him peace. And I hope that you, the core of you, may outweigh your mistakes. I let my hand rest on the stone, placed here by pagans for reasons that we might never understand, and we begin our walk back to the cars. The afternoon fades and the magic is broken. But I will return to this place, the stone and the trees, and maybe I will find a stag beetle amongst the decaying wood, that brings new life from the earth.

It seems as if you and I are forever connected to water. The giver of life welcomes your death and my leaking eyes. The boat moves lazily along parched, dusty banks, interspersed by tall palms and the lush green of small fields, nestled as closely as possible to the river.

How often have we talked about this journey, this exploration of truth? How often did we wish to touch ancient stones and maybe, just maybe absorb something of the history hidden in their pores? My fingers closed around the small bottle try to remember you skin. Sometimes, I fear that I have lost the memory of your voice, your smell, that I might lose you completely, can no longer keep you alive. Now, just at this moment more than ever, I need you alive, with me, next to me. My eyes are tired of seeing for both of us. And yet, we are travelling, endlessly visiting the world, places, people, making memories that will bind us together, even if I have to make them on my own.

I have learned much on our travels. I have learned that people are kind, even if they don't always understand. I have learned that my body functions and seems to exist, whilst my soul has long flown with yours. I have learned that I will never again occupy the whole expanse of my bed and that my tears can be reserved for the times when I am on my own. I have re-learned to listen to music and travel to places that I have long left. I have learned that I can negotiate the outside world without panic and fear. And most importantly, I have learned that I can keep promises, however big and impossible they seem.

The boat's engine falls silent, and the river lies still in the early evening light. Tonight, my Darling, I will leave you for the first time amongst the dust of history in this country. Hidden amongst the carved stones, one of your dreams will be complete. I cover my head and my shoulders, respecting Gods that have ceased to exist an eternity ago. Replaced, forgotten, buried under years of sand and erased from memory because the new Gods would not tolerate what came before. How can any God be so insecure and imperfect that it is necessary to obliterate others? But ultimately, I cannot imagine, that they really need temples and ceremonies. At his moment, I pray silently that your heart has been found to be pure when weighed against the feather and that your soul has found a peaceful place to rest. I pray that Maat can see that all your neglect, your cruelty, your mistakes were just that. Mistakes made because the little beaten, unnurtured creature inside of you had not been able to grow.

Touching the stones in the twilight, the heat of the day radiates into my skin. I release you from your glass vessel and my hand rests for a while on the small pile of greyish powder that I am going to leave in the space where an ancient stone once was. This now, this moment, mingles with that last breath you took. No speeches, no last words, leaving me with nothing but a promise to keep. My beautiful emperor, proud and unbending like the columns of yellow sandstone glowing around me in the failing light. Mass of contradictions, full of pain and only finding peace when it was too late. The Nile, unruffled and calm swallows the sun as it has done for an eternity.

Sara, who has distracted our guide, takes my hand and we leave you amongst the ruins of a kingdom that once seemed indestructible. We only now realise that my mission might be not always as private and benign. Months ago, at the beginning of our travels, I had checked and made sure that I could fly with you in my pockets. People have been understanding and kind. But in this place, with its mixture of old and new beliefs, guards with guns watch our every move. And leaving or taking anything from these sites, is an interference too far. After centuries of changing Gods and rituals, one truth has remained unchanged. After death, you still need your body and cremations is literally unheard of. The preservation of the body is a sacred duty. Have I unwittingly not only failed to keep you alive, but also burned all of your chances of an afterlife? Your body, in its present from is an affront to the rites of those, whose temples we visit. And even worse, me leaving you here is beyond what might be considered to be respectful. Sara and I have realised that it is nearly impossible to find private moments amongst the stones. The guide is dedicated to staying with us and explain the different features of these holy places; I am trying hard to escape from his view. Trying to find a moment, a crack in the stones without being seen. How is a body complete if the brain is removed? Mummies, their bandages turning to dust in daylight, with their hearts in place, dried bodies hidden in tombs more ornate than palaces, seem to be a strange choice for rebirth.

I stumble away from the temple, which leaves me strangely untouched. Only your presence here, the hope that I have hidden you well enough from the winds and the sand, make the place somewhere where I leave roots behind. I realise that I need to explain to the guide why I am here. He is our defence against guards, eternally keen to take photos for us, only mentioning money later; against the children and street sellers who try to bar our way towards places of interest. I need to explain the inexplicable, a promise that suddenly seems empty and pointless.

The tall frame of the guide seems to shrink during my somewhat inept attempt to make him understand Us. He explains that neither the ancients not the present inhabitants of this mystical land that makes a poor living from strange travellers, could possibly encompass the idea of a dead man travelling in his wife's pockets only to be abandoned in ancient stones. But, in the end he seems to accept the bizarre importance of my travels and promises that we will have some time alone at every temple we visit. However, he warns of the guards with machine guns, who despite all their friendliness take the protection of the old stones very seriously. I nod. A small step forward. Explaining Us has become a little easier and I blush less.

I have a distinct goal, a space, where you will be amongst those who are your equal, were you rightfully need to rest. I will claim your place amongst the kings and queens.

Do you think they cried, screamed, felt cut by losses like ours? The people, who built these temples into the sand, near the lush green abundance of the riverbanks, did they love and wondered, trying to hold on to some hope that those lost might return. They must have done. Humanity, in the end is governed by love and birth, by death and loss.

How firm was their belief in this magical afterlife, which somehow seemed to retain the structures and privileges of this earth? Did the grace of their gods really depend on the lavishness of temples and worship? I am sure of little, but I am certain that there must have been the feet of other women like me, wandering around these sandy paths, lost in this all-encompassing, all-consuming pain. Thinking of the lone figure of the Albanian women, chopping wood at the foot of the barren hills, I feel connected to this army of women, who have walked alone and without hope.

Somehow, the light over the river, softened by purple and pink haziness, allows me to believe in magic. It reminds me of the sunsets above Prague, bathed in music and footsteps echoing on cobbled stones. It is early and the heat of the day to come is still only a slight promise, whilst Ra begins his journey to the zenith. The colours of the early morning are gentle but will soon change into the harsh ochre of the day. The light plays on the water and from somewhere unseen, the call to prayer echoes across the river. Last night, I tried to understand why Egyptians are not African and what they would have made of your skin. It seems that the Greeks, who ruled this endless expanse of sand for such a long time, were seduced by the mysterious culture but still could not create sculptures of the Gods correctly. The greatest queen a foreigner and yet readily absorbed into the narrative. A land gently occupied by several cultures and still holding on to its essence. Taxes owed measured by the height of the river. The same tools used today to excavate ancestors, as used by them to build their temples and work their fields. Temples for Gods, whom nobody believes in, protected by guards with guns. I visit the temples with a veil drawn tightly around my head and my shoulders. My defence against people, who try to make a living and stop me from taking my dead to rest in their monuments.

We take a raggedy boat to the small island, bathed in glimmering heat and the new home of an old temple. With my head and shoulders covered, I am wondering whom I am respecting. When this temple was built, people like you and me would not have been allowed to go to the inner spaces, now I am touching the stones and hide you in the cracks with the best views. I am not sure if the Ancients required women to veil, but I know the Islamic women of Egypt do. Not all are veiled, but all will cover their shoulders and their arms as a mark of respect when they visit places of worship. This temple belongs to a faith that has long since died and to Gods that have lost their power. And yet, we are expected to show respect in these formerly holy places. This particular temple has been moved, so that it might not disappear amongst the new expanse of water created by the Aswan Dam. How can it still hold its magical powers when it is no longer at the site it was created for? How can the sun have the same power to cast shadows that brought messages to the priests when the angles have changed and the plants around the temple are feed by a different expanse of water? I think, you and I, during all those weeks of researching, exploring and planning, have been asking the wrong questions. We concentrated so hard on the purpose of the ancient monuments, their meaning and the way they could have been constructed. We somehow imagined we would visit these places, explored the stones with our skin on our own, in peace and would find some clarity and understanding of the Ancients. The truth, my truth as I feel it now, squatting in the sand under a temple arch and staring at the water, is very different. I am wondering less about the Ancients and their tools and more about how the living manage to exist in a frozen world, preserving temples and statues to people who are as strange and mysterious to them as they are to me. Like for Us, the dead are more important than the living, here they provide income and keep people alive; in me, my promise to you keeps me somehow traveling forwards. Quite befittingly, this place, this temple, on its original island had been the last place the old religions were followed, the ancient rites performed. When Christianity and later Islam crowded out the old gods and allowed their statues to be covered by sand, these stones protected the last monks and priests of the dying faith.

I leave you behind in a crack in the yellow stone, rest my hand on the earth that seems to be more dust than soil and rescue Sara from an armed guard, who has taken a photo of her and is now looking for payment. You would have been upset, would have maybe raised your voice a little. But as things are, in the here and now, I have to leave a small amount of ash, and feel very uncertain about everything. Sometimes I wish you could see our travels, and at other times, I think it would be better if you had no idea what is happening in this world you have left. I need you to be happy and warm and safe and not worried about the mess and the confusion you have left behind.

Today, my Darling, we will visit the place we had looked forward to more than many others. Today, my Emperor, I will lay you to rest amongst ancient kings and queens. Only slowly, it dawns on me, how little sense our travels might make to others, and that it might even be unwelcome and risky. Just how monumental the gulf between Us and the rest of the world has become. On our way, cool in the coach, crossing a bridge from the east to the west bank of the river, I see my first sheep in this country and smile. I want to bury my face in their fleeces and breathe in the musty smell of sunshine and grass. Although the land is arid, the soil poor and sandy, there must be enough for them to graze and survive. The legs of sheep are fragile and seem to be unsuitable to carry those sturdy bodies. I think of my sheep at home and the lush pasture that leaves them spoilt for choice. They can rest in shade and shelter under trees, they have my hands running through their curls and scratch behind their ears. Their way of running towards me, shaking their heads in recognition and pushing their noses into my pockets. Laying in the high grass with them, resting and staring at the clouds, gives me peace; their warm breath on my shoulders lets me forget for a little while. Surrounded by grass, heavy, gentle animals and dragonflies from the pond across the path, I can find something of the old me. These sheep are hardier, sturdier and more resigned to the hot sun and the poor ground. Their legs are not as long as those I have seen in the Albanian mountains, their bodies leaner, but they all bear the same expression of purpose and watchfulness. With their strangely shaped eyes, they can see what is happening behind them without having to turn their heads. My sheep at home know my voice and the sound of my car over the sound of other engines. They are wild and domesticated at the same time and feel very familiar to me.

The air in the valley of the kings is still, hot and silent. Somehow it feels like wandering amongst the high buildings of a modern city at night; or possibly the approach to a disused quarry, reminding me of the edges of a place where they used to quarry gypsum when I was a child and where we harvested elderberries in the autumn. My mother filled the flat with the sweet smell of boiling elderberries whilst producing bottle after bottle of juice for the winter. There is a strange air of abandoned industriousness. I expected majestic gravitas and find dust.

A group of Americans, loud and full of boisterous life seem to have the same destinations that we have chosen. We are allowed to visit 3 of the tombs and we made our choice based on the difficulty of the descent into the underworld. A wizen man stamps our tickets to ensure that we do not make more than the allocated visits. He also asks for change in any currency, but we are used to this now and just smile at him. He smiles back, probably not having expected success and not disappointed. We touch stone walls, cool and thick after the glaring light outside, make our way on wooden walkways deeper and deeper into caves under the desert sand. The people laid to rest here needed a lot of space and gifts for their journeys to the afterlife. I wonder about the others, people without title and status. The unpreserved, unfound, left in shallower places. As in all tombs and temples along the Nile, guards keep a watchful eye on visitors, making my mission difficult. I struggle to really see the beauty around me, appreciate the work, the pictures and carvings of this underground palace. Concentrating hard on finding the right place, the regal companion who might be worthy of you, whilst at the same time needing to find a moment of privacy and by default safety. In the end, I manage to drop a little of you into one of the chambers, one of the places where a pharaoh has rested. One from the New Kingdom, closest to our time. Powerful and reigning for nearly 30 years, the warrior king seems to be a fitting host for you. Sara, irritated by the American youths starts to mutter under her breath and we begin our ascent back into the sun and the heat. I am glad that we visited early during the day, before the sun would bake the earth and make my head spin. Close to what is now your tomb, we find a shop, selling trinkets and coffee.

Egyptian coffee is strong and sweet. I opt for tea sit, on the floor, leaning against the wall of the building. From here, I can see the rise and fall of the barren landscape, the sun and the natural pyramid shape overshadowing the valley. Somehow it occurs to me that, if Egypt would serve alcohol, and if you were with me now, we would sit here, with you gulping whiskey and blinking into the sun. Irreverent, numb you, would love this exact spot, this place more than any other. I leave a little of you here, just here, in your place, in a place I will remember forever; encapsulating you more than the tomb or the ancient stones and wonders. My dress is covered in dust and sand and Sara takes a picture of me, sitting comfortably next to you and this wall, my headscarf hiding my hair and my fingers digging into the soil. I take a little of the sand with me, replacing you with something that is indistinguishable from your ashes in the little glass bottle. Although we might not come from the earth at the beginning, we become part of it after we stop breathing and thinking and dreaming. From dust to dust, I have to laugh at the thought that you and the dust in the valley of kings are now one and nobody could tell the difference. That you rest at the wall of what might be a Mexican bodega seems strangely fitting and yet absurdly disrespectful.

At the mortuary temple of Hatshepsut, we are reminded that dysfunctionality and squabbles amongst families are as old as humanity. The stepson of this powerful and glorious ruler tried to eradicate her from history. And although he did not succeed completely, I wonder if anything has really changed when it comes to the delicate balance of love and power, of biological and other kin. I think of my children and yours, of the web of relationships and hurt inflicted unwittingly and without malice. Of the wounds that are the inheritance of our children and those we have received from our parents. The sins of our fathers, the continuation of habits and neglect have been present even then, in the same way as they are now.

I sit on the terrace in front of the enormous collection of columns, designed to impress, to be a monument of a dead ruler. Power to be demonstrated even after the queen had found her hidden resting place. Sara and I have grown tired and weary, the adrenaline of the last hours slowly retreating, leaves us hollow. We take a drink in the restaurant, whilst we are waiting for the coach and the guide to return and Sara shares her painkillers with one of the waiters, who complains about a headache. The mundane, the everyday present even in the grandest of settings. People, their shared worries, their humanity and compassion as well as their greed, their misunderstandings and jealousies have not changed. The waiter waives as we leave and I look back at the place that you now share with Ramses III, feeling somehow proud.

Luxor basks in the early morning purples. I watch the silent giants of the air, floating gently across the sky, taking tourists to experience the landscape from above. I long to be on one of those balloons, being able to touch the mist and let you fly from a great height. The mist over the river is slowly lifting as we begin the last day of this journey. One more day to show you the country you dreamt of so many times. One more temple full of statues and columns, some of which our guide dismisses as too Greek. He points at carvings that are not sufficiently Egyptian, despite the fact that the Aegean descendants ruled this place for nearly 300 years and everyone I quizzed defines themselves as non-African. It is impossible for me to understand this amalgamation of Gods, beliefs, traditions that have somehow merged into this living museum where the role of the living is unclear. The dead kings and queens overshadow everything, bring in people like us to sustain the living, who might have to vacate their homes if someone discovers monuments buried under their flimsy houses. Living spaces remain unkempt to polish monuments and alleys of sphinxes. When houses eventually deteriorate past repair, the inhabitants are moved to make space for more buried treasures. I struggle with the idea that seemingly nobody has remembered the holy places for long enough for them to get covered by desert sand and new houses, and yet they now, devoid of real meaning, have become the centre of everything.

When I find the mosque nestling in the temple of Luxor, slightly raised above the ancient Gods, very much in use amongst the beautiful remains of ancient stone, I have to smile. And more confusion, when we see the early Christian scenes on a temple wall, plastered over the old and repurposed to a different faith that eventually came to dominate and destroy the old systems. Three deities at ease with each other, whilst their follower squabble and seeking dominance. And not for the first time, I am unsure what is worth preserving, the old stone underneath or the frescos of later times? I sit, exhausted by thought, in the shadow of the massive walls and wonder, not for the first time, if you and I did not explore the wrong things, asked somewhat irrelevant questions. We asked how and why these buildings came into being, we did not ask about the daily life of those who are not recorded and who somehow drifted from faith to faith, from ruler to ruler, whilst tending the same sheep and used the same utensils as today. The builders, whose hands made all this possible, the shepherds and farmers, the widows and their children, we should have wondered about them, maybe we could have understood them better than those who rule and demonstrate their power through monuments. So many new questions, no answers, no enlightenment from the stones, whilst Ra still drowns every night and returns in the morning, making us marvel at life and the rebirth of colours.

My hope that the guard might be distracted has been misplaced. I know he has been watching us for some time, but as we have to leave soon, and I have found the place I want you to inhabit. So, I have to use the moment when his eyes are diverted and place you in a small hollow within the stone. Must not appear to hurry away, must not look guilty of anything. But of course, his path towards your hiding place and mine towards the exit, cross and our eyes meet for a second. I join Sara, who has found a dog looking forlorn in the late morning sun. And of course, I turn to watch the movements of the guard. His hand is looking for something in your resting place, but he cannot find you. Dust and ashes are too similar, mingled in the small, dark place and he looks puzzled. Stares at me, sure that I have done something untoward, but not being able to work out what it is. Sara, sharing her last water with the dog, glares at a group of guards, demanding that the thin animal should be fed and cared for. Our guide tries to move us away, assuring her that the men will share their lunch with the creature that has made this place his home. I am not sure that I believe him but echo his words.

Our long-suffering guide takes his leave and like the teachers of my former life, he appears relieved to escape from my endless questions. Have you and I succeeded in our mission to find answers? Will you understand this place better now, being part of the stones and the sand? Will you ponder at night over the mysteries humans create? Do you still believe in some other-worldly influence over the capabilities of ancient builders or grieve over the stray animals, former holy creatures in their own right? Animals loved you. Even the angriest of dogs would playfully follow your hands and lick the salt off your skin. That gives me hope. If there is a soul, if there is some other place, if your heart is placed on the scales against the white feather, surely the judging powers will see you through the eyes of the innocent, nature, the animals that trusted you. The harm you did was borne from your own pain and you paid the price in full. And I take my place in the endless row of invisible women with empty spaces right in the middle of them. Functioning, laughing, surviving, steely creatures searching for purpose. Disposed queens with their faces removed from the stone that was meant to make them eternal. Suddenly I realise that I have not seen any women during our visit here. Tourists, yes, but no women on the street, during their daily tasks, making a living, tending sheep or fields. They are not passengers or drivers on the endless throng of scooters and cars, they are not walking through the heat with heavy bags full of fruit and bread. And with that, I am suddenly sure that we have seen only a small strip of this river, reserved to be exhibited and photographed. That there must be more land that holds answers to some of my questions. We have seen the dead, the extinct, the long distant past; those, who are now your people, exist in your realm. And I hover between these places, between the lost you and those whose hearts are still beating in the glaring, merciless sun.

Sara and I cry as we empty the remaining parts of you into the Nile, flowing free, maybe even encountering a crocodile, maybe making your way all the way to the sea. I will return to the North, for us to explore the pyramids and for you to join the sand dunes, forever changing shape and view. I love you, as you were, before and during the pandemic, during our time in the cottage, when you shouted at the beach, when we searched for treasure and a way to survive. I love you as you were during our last seven weeks, and I love the boy deep inside of you. Maybe that, just that is your immortality. Our journey, our travels, maybe they are your legacy. But they will disappear with me and my memories.

They will fly away with your ashes and decay with the monuments I have made your home. Only the water will survive and the trees, in their younger versions, will still keep you safe. I hold Sara's hand and feel old.

At the airport, on our way home, it really becomes clear, just how close you and I have sailed to the wind. Our travels are not always welcome, even less understood. Security is paramount in a country, thar inhabits part of a region full of enemies, unseen, changing and shifting, adding more difficulties to an already precarious life. Passports stamped and re-stamped, examined, checked and pondered over. Bags emptied, hastily re-packed and emptied again. Endless checkpoints and security questions. And after every examination, we think we might have turned the last corner to the gates. The need for safety and security is understandable and we submit to every question with a clear conscious. Until the last moment – a tall, determined looking young man as dusted our phones for explosives and examines my bags again. He stumbles across the tiny glass vessel with sand from the Valley of Kings. His eyes grow dark and alert. And then he asks the dreaded question. He wants to know if the bottle contains human remains. I blush, but I can assure him that this is just sand, sand from one of the holy places. His body tenses. He remains inscrutable and turns the offending item in his hand, obviously considering a closer inspection and testing of the pale grey grains that are so important to me that I carry them next to my toothbrush in my bag. He relents and hands the bottle back to me.

I flee, join Sara at the gate and we make our way to a smoking area. You and I, we have been lucky that this young man was not in charge of checking when we arrived. Who knows what the response might have been if he had discovered you? And you would have been unable to rescue me. You, who had scant disregards for rules, were always worried about my need to climb fences and explore places we were not supposed to enter. You always tried to hold me back and then waited with a resigned smile, close enough to catch me if I should slip. I confused you with my need to enter rusty, disused, abandoned places, but you never disapproved or tried to stop me. Just shrugged your shoulders, smiled, had a cigarette, a drink and waited. And I never disapproved of your drinking and gambling, of your retreats into a rabbit hole of dreams, where I could not follow. Just waited for you to re-emerge, ready to be held.

Travelling with your Ashes

The memory of your skin held in my fingertips is growing fainter, however hard I try to hold onto all the small moments that now only exist in me. I am wearing less black, but any plan for the future is hazy and rejected as soon as it appears. The pain has become bearable, but deeper, encapsulated somewhere in me; hidden away, to be released only when I am on my own. The living claim my attention, demand care and consideration, often more than I can give. I am in a permanent state of exhaustion, fighting my way between the different parts of me. The words from my mouth compete with those in my thoughts. Slowly, I do things, visit places that were important to us. I still pick up things you would have liked, only to set them down again as if my skin had been burned. And still we travel, still I touch the top of your urn every morning. Many of my sensibilities have changed. Your ashes are just that, a collection of light grey, oily grains. A symbol, not a person. You are in my soul, in my memory, in me, you are not in that urn. Not the you that matters, not your smile, your tears – not you. I had a pendant made from your ashes, for your angel sister. The next best thing to the diamonds you had wanted to become. There was only very little ash needed, but it required to be posted. Not long ago, I stared at the urn, unable to open the lid, to cope with your changed shape; accept that is all I am left with of our future. I have learned to decanter the grains into small bottles, balloons and rubber ducks; taking a small amount and place it in the discreet bag designed for the purpose is no longer difficult. I struggle more with my visit to the post office in the village where we started our journey and that supplied your bottles during the pandemic. Picturesque core of the village that is forever grows tentacles of modern estates with box houses and where incomers are still considered with suspicion and shunned in the pub. You caused more than a little confusion, and often came home, talking of stares on the train, which only lessened once you passed Gatwick. On your return journey, you did not notice maybe because you were simply too drunk and often asleep.

But over time, especially during lockdown, people grew used to the sight of your slight frame, gliding through the village. They stopped and talked, especially about the cat. My redhaired little friend, ancient even then, had made the whole village his home. He had different names in different houses and only came home when he had exploited the goodwill all the way down to the village square and the shop.

Apart from some close friends, nobody here knows what has happened and I feel safe when I take the envelope into the shop that doubles as the village post office. The young man behind the counter remembers me, smiles and begins the process of sending you on your first journey in an envelope. Everything ordinary, although something in me expects you to stand behind me, asking for a bottle of Jack Daniels. An ordinary letter to an ordinary address. Until the young man asks something I did not expect. He needs to know the contents of the padded envelope in his hand, now with the stamp attached. My brain scrambles for an acceptable answer, but the only thing that I can think of is you. 'My husband', my voice sounds as crazy as the words, and I can see his face contort a little. He stares at me and I am sure that his brain experiences equal pointless torment as mine just seconds ago. 'I have never posted a person before,' is the result of his struggles and somehow, we both laugh. I am not sure if he remembers you but think it likely. You are hard to forget.

He is slightly more careful than he would normally be when he places you in the grey, waterproof sack that will take you and the rest of the mail of this day away. What surprises me is that neither of us are embarrassed and that there was no need for condolences and pretend sorrow. You will arrive at your angel's sister's home in ten days' time and give her some small piece or solace. I leave the shop, stop and take in the square, with my feet wanting to take the familiar path up the hill towards the cottage. Instead, I open the door to the car and burst into uncontrollable tears, hiding my face in the steering wheel.

Why did we take the news so calmly; why did we accept that we had no other options than to go home and make the best of the last few weeks we had been given? I had not expected the diagnosis to be so final, the prognosis being what it was. And yet, that moment, when the enormity of an event hits you, physically touches you, did not come. Did you know, expect, foresee? We talked about our fears, our darkest dreams, talked about treatments and what you would accept; we did not talk about the possibility that we would lose each other, that there would be no offer of treatment and hope. We did not talk about this moment, when I am walking on my own through a world that is bereft of you and Us, that is empty and cold. We talked about me taking you travelling, but not about me and my tears. We took every day as a gift, to be filled with love and mischief. And when you said that you were winning this uneven, unfair fight against the enemy growing inside of you, we both knew that it was illusion that made the nights easier for both of us.

Gill, a friend of many years, who cries with me and for you, meets me outside of the cathedral. One morning, what now seems to be an eternity ago, when she visited us in the cottage and the cat was home for breakfast, she sat on our bed and spoke to you about drink. Open and honestly, not from experience but with compassion. You smiled and accepted her care with good grace. But it took another seven months until you decided that you did not need your numbness anymore. Would things be different today if I had spoken about it more; if it had really worried me enough to ask you to do something, to change your habits; to become a different kind of demon tamer? Gill, with her eloquent hands and a head full of hopes has travelled with me for a long time now. I used to teach her sons, played with them in my language, long before my daughters were born. Somehow, she has always been there, even if we did not see each other for many months between respective visits. Practical, organised Gill, powerful, without frills, full of internal struggles and pain, holds me for a while and her warmth seeps into my cold, clammy soul. I want to leave you here, in the cathedral, at the spot where my beautiful friend, who paints dead trees and the faces that inhabit his nightmares, once exhibited his paintings. You and I stood, mesmerised, in front of the canvass and you understood the struggle in every stroke of his paintings. Later, you fell in love with the tree at the end of our bed that had been destined for the fire, when painting trees and barbed wire landscapes was no longer enough to quell the voices in my friend's soul. You had touched the paint and become one with the loneliness of the unwanted, misunderstood of this earth. We wandered, our hands entwined, across the cold flagstones and talked about the universe and the strange twists of genetics and experience that create people like us. Neither God nor any other eternal being would have felt at home in this dark place full of plaques and the bones of those considered worthy of resting in glorious stone coffins. We stopped a while in front of Gustav Holst's memorial, discussing his origins and only settled the argument about the discrepancy between his name and his nationality when we returned to the cottage and were able to research the issue.

And today, when I am ready to re-visit this place and leave you at the spot where we stood, not even two years ago, the doors to the cathedral are locked. Closed to the public, reserved for ordinations, proud parents and solemn young men in black frocks swarm across the space. The cathedral refuses to accept you to rest amongst the dignitaries and wealthy. The cloister walk to the side of the main building is lined with barred openings, surrounding a garden of exceptional peace amongst all the pomp the gothic builders employed to glorify the deity. Gill and I sit on one of the ledges, staring onto the grass and trying to evade the gazes of those who hurry towards church doors and celebrations. In the end, there is a quiet moment, a second, a heartbeat, really and my hand stretches through the iron bars, spilling the ash onto the grass. I have to smile. Surely. nobody is allowed to walk on those perfect green blades. Mischief, you and I can still create mischief.

My mind wanders back to hot temples along the bank of the Nile. No different; those, who want to be remembered, want to be eternal, align themselves with the Gods, and create buildings, forbidding and imposing, rising into the sky, visible from miles away and dwarfing all living things. And yet, unlike these stone palaces, the universe gives us grass and trees, lakes and the wild sea, holding and giving life. So, in a way, I am glad that you float amongst the grass and the roses, rather than the polished stone floor on the inside of the cathedral. Here, you will see the seasons; you can breathe and wander; and the wind can play with the grains under a full moon, far away from pomp and ceremony.

And maybe we were right all along. Everything happens when and how it is meant to happen. Maybe that is the reason why we did not question, cried of despaired when they told us that there was nothing anyone could do of us. Maybe we were so calm, because we accepted that we could not change the course of the universe. But now, at this moment, with Gill holding my hand, I feel unquenchable anger with the Gods, the universe and any other power that there might be. I can accept that you had to leave on the wings of the storm when you did. I can accept that you had that peaceful moment when you had to do nothing other than to stop breathing. I can accept that that day, that moment was part of the plan, the blueprint that I cannot understand. What I can not accept, not embrace, is that I had to stay behind, without purpose and sense. That I have stumble on, carrying your ashes under this sky, is unbearably unjust.

Gill begins her return journey to Aylesbury and I sit for a while next to the chair in the hall, staring at your shoes, your jacket, still waiting for a sign and some clarity.

My feet touch the water, my hands rest on the grey stones that protect the shore. In the distance, ships full of cargo seem to wait for permission to move. Although I know better, I wonder if these are the same freighters I watch from the Albanian beaches. But the water under my feet is not the Aegean, this is the Black Sea and if I were to take a direct route across the water, I would find myself in the war in Ukraine. What would you think about this event, that both of us thought impossible? Where are the words you would say now, on this shore, with one of the most confusing cities on earth behind us and the sun playing on the waves around the resting ships?

What would you say to this brother of yours, to the day exactly a year younger than you, who sits next to me? He loves his cats, rescued and nurtured back to health and glossy coats. At this moment, he seems nothing like you, nothing to remind me of you. Apart from his words retelling events that you shared, an eternity ago. But like with all witnesses, the same moments have left different imprints on both of you. You have drawn different conclusions, took different paths. Your body stayed where it felt familiar, where you knew the pain and the loneliness, but kept your soul comfortably numb. He left, stretched the distance between himself and the past, but kept his mind clear. He tells of young boys and the father he perceived as simply strict and unpredictable, whilst you suffered and grew into the wounded young man who searched so haplessly for love and belonging. Your soul, always fragile, hidden behind a coat of steel, clung onto the dark dreams and yet, unable to separate the invisible chains, stayed and looked for approval and apologies that never came. You share a cough and I worry for him. Your brother, who does not resemble you, did not know about your drinking, just about your other addictions and is not really surprised. He knew you as a gambler, who lost more than you won; as a petty thief and wayward youth. The only one not taken into care, who evaded capture by helpful hands. Does he love you? I am not asking him, and in the end it does not matter. He has agreed to meet me, in this city, half European, half Asian, half modern high-rising glass palaces, half cobbled stones lined with basement sweatshops. That is enough for me. He is sitting next to Us, holding a little of you in his hands. And we let you go; let you sail towards the unmoving ships, drifting the other side of the sea or some other place along the same shore. Relationships, families, these complex, intricately webs of emotions, rejection and love, are quite unfathomable to me. Words used to sow suspicion, pain and confusion might have been uttered to breathe some kind of truth and yet, they widen gaps and draw the nets tighter until breathing becomes impossible. The intentions amongst clans are probably loving and wonderful, but bring only hurt and alienation.

Like your brother, I found it easier to leave, to supplement the internal distance with geographical separation. In truth, he knows as little about you as I do about my own sister. Here, on the stones along the water's edge, I find only some distant memories of your childhood, confirming what you have relived in your nightmares and shared with me. I also find more recent events, witnessed from a distance, speculations and assumptions about your family and the inevitable feuds amongst people, who neither know each other well, nor ever felt complete in themselves. I am trying hard to fit pieces together, place names next to the few faces of those I have met. Why do people inflict this unbearable pain on each other and then cry at the funerals of those they have hurt? Why did you have the need to make peace with those who wounded you so deeply? What changed during those last weeks? You found peace and I am glad. But has that really changed the dynamics of hurt and misplaced righteousness inhabited by the living? Your brother opens the small bottle and we let you go into the sea. Another set of waves for you to explore, to ride on into some strange freedom that I envy.

I have another goal in this city. Holy ground, pink walls and blue roofs, across the impressive plaza from the Blue Mosque, the Hagia Sophia, torn between Orthodox and Islam. Many years ago, not much more than a child then, I visited this place, wandered through the cobblestoned streets and jumped from Asia to Europe in the middle of a red bridge. Long before I discovered my love for doors, I marvelled at the remains of many different cultures mingling in the streets of a city that had once ruled a large part of the world and gave us coffee and carpets. A city that taught me backgammon and gave me a first glimpse of minarets bathed in hazy blue and pink hues. Fascinated then as now, by men pulling carts filled with carpets and fridges, with rubbish and leather, up the narrow cobblestoned streets. Intrigued by a proud people, who once glittered and dominated, and whom I met later in the guise of those who came to work in my country. Unsettled, uprooted, no longer part of one culture and not yet part of the other. The death of empires seems to be followed by a deeper loss than might have been inflicted without previous glory. People, like countries, proud of a glorious past and unsure about the present, stumble through their daily lives with resentment and the search for strong leaders, who promise the unachievable. Without Us, without all that hope and love, I would not being able to miss you quite as deeply as I do. Without colonies and empires as the foundation of pride, and lost over time, some cultures might have continued to blossom and flourish and not suddenly felt defeated and deprived. Without the travels of my youth, I might not miss people and places who have crossed my path. I suddenly feel poorer for the richness of my life.

Your brother questions the wisdom of my plan to leave you at the Blue Mosque, I insist that you and I are accomplished breakers of convention and laws. His face adopts a worried expression when I tell him about our Egyptian adventures. Apparently, this area is heavily policed, and any form of littering might land Us in trouble. He stands a long way apart from me, pretending to take a picture, looking out for plain clothed police. And I say good-bye again to you, leaving you in a crack next to some steps leading up to the mosque. You, who did not hold with religions or gods, resting in so many places holy to others, seems somewhat misplaced, but I am sure that you would appreciate the settings and the history you are now part of. Invading spaces that would not welcome you, with your wry smile and challenging arms outstretched against their walls. Were you immune to rules and ultimately free and strong, or shackled forever by your demons, forced to stand by and watch the world from a distance?

Your brother, the only left of a group of three close in age, a stranger to me and maybe even to you, walks next to me across the piazza amongst flocks of tourists. A stranger, and yet somehow bound to me by your existence. He now has some small bottles in his pockets to take you to the Bosporus and places that mean something to him. Although, I fear that he might not be sentimental enough to name such sanctuaries, I hope that he has them in his heart and will visit them with you. He might even talk to you, as you have not been able to do for years.

Over dinner, we talk, easily and amicably. When he speaks about politics and the world, he grows animated and for brief moments, I can see a little of you and I am glad. You share many opinions and judgements and I find it strangely comforting to listen to him. Away from your history, from kin and responsibility and pain, he is sure-footed and wise. I wonder if his exile is a lonely place, only inhabited by music and cats. Not happy and not unhappy, comfortably numb without distractions and drink. I would like to ask him about his life, his feelings, his fears and hopes, but he is not a man who invites questions.

He walks me slowly back to my hotel. Clearly not a great walker, nor particularly familiar with the old part of this city, he struggles at times. I realise that I have lost my lighter as well as the belt of my coat, and we enter one of the many basements to buy matches. Feeling strangely safe and familiar, I climb the steep pavements of the old town and feel at home. Away from the modern city, dominated by glass and glittering surfaces, away from the cleanliness outside of the mosques, away from the lights of restaurants and phone flashes, deep in the shadows, I am taken back many years. Back to being the young girl full of hope, travelling on the wind and the waves, being engulfed by strange voices and smells.

The basement sweatshops are bathed in light, and I can watch men sewing leather into bags and belts, whilst others pull large carts full of carpets and fruit through the warm air; the grandsons of those I watched so many years ago. Some pull discarded plastic and paper to unknown places. The women in this part of the city wear scarfs and smile. Back at my hotel, your brother leaves and as he walks away, I feel sadness for him and his long journey to another part of town. I feel sadness for the three little boys, playing football on the grass, unaware what life has in store for them and how early two of them will leave and fly on the wind. You and Anton died within ten days of each other. United in life by your kidneys, united in death, leaving just one brother of your generation behind. When Anton died, your kidney, deep in his body, died with him and at that moment, I knew that you would not be with me for much longer. I wish you had a chance to talk and walk with your brother and me through the balmy night air and find closeness in shared history.

All I could bring him are small bottles with ashes and my memories of you. I can tell him that you had a good death, that your final moments were free of pain and struggle. I leave him with the promise to visit your mother's grave and watch him walking down the hill. Strangers, who somehow became part each other's stories, not quite kin, not friends, not close and yet of importance.

I have a last cigarette on the terrace in front of the hotel, the street still busy, cobbles glistening with a hint of drizzle that makes the air smell fresh and dusty at the same time. Tomorrow, I will make my long way through the confusing, crawling traffic of Istanbul, back to the airport. Having completed another step of our journey without destination or end point. All I know is that I will come back to explore the wonderful doors and walls of this city that is neither one thing nor another. I am not sure, if I will ever see your brother again, but I am glad that we met and shared an afternoon with you in our pockets.

I am retracing our steps, slowly, thoughtfully driving north from the sea. Many years were spent in a landlocked place that left me fighting for breath. Some were happy, some were not, but during every second, I missed the sea. My daughters were born here, my son met his wife. Wonderful memories of friendship and rainbows in the garden mingle with sadness and unfulfilled dreams. As I cross through the town that was my home for so long, I avoid the street, the house, the bitterness for a while longer and continue towards the Chiltern hills. Green, sweeping landscape patrolled in elegant circles by red kites. When my son was four years old and the wind dropped us in this alien land, there were hardly any of these majestic birds. Now they are so numerous that people are warned of the danger to small pets.

I make my way up to the golden ball, overlooking two valleys, the town and Dashwood's house. The bronze age cave under the church and the mausoleum has a dark reputation. Rumours of orgies and black magic kept the peasants away, hiding in their small houses in the village, where now heavy traffic makes windows shake and foundations crumble. Pagans have used this site and worshipped the sun, and the air is still filled with heavy shadows of poverty and failed harvests. Not long ago, you and I sat in the long grass and watched the clouds from this place close to the sky and far away from the once prosperous town that fashioned a fortune from chairs. I take your small bottle from my pocket and release your ashes into the wind. Not the mausoleum for you, not this memorial to privilege and cruelty. You will be free with the kites, flying across the gentle expanse of land, surveying the seasons and watch snow settling on the fields, where I once threw snowballs at my children and wandered around gravestones with my dog.

We are on our way to wave good-bye to an old friend. Rosa, once closer to me than any sister; my Spanish friend with the broad smile and unruly hair. We were neighbours once, shared the same road in the valley below, two foreigners lost amongst cultures. Someho

w both of us had managed to land in this town, once home to sturdy woodworkers and joiners, now a replica of Lahore. A community that struggled with us, with our otherness; a community that had built a fortress of semis, defending familiar traditions against the host country. No clashes, no fight for superiority, just a gentle wave of industrious incomers changing the landscape. Slowly, headscarves replaced hairpins and the mosque became the centre daily routines. All that had happened imperceptible, before we arrived and both, Rosa and I, tried to settle into two different cultures, both alien from our own. Our children shared the walk to school and afternoons in the garden. Eventually, Rosa left, moving further and further away, until we lost touch. I stayed, learned to prepare curry and discuss the Quran with the imam. Every Christmas, the children of our street waited for me to bring home the tree and it was decorated and redecorated by tiny hands until most of the needles had fallen and covered the floor. My son learned two languages at the same time, growing fluent in both and lost his own. I have been told that his Punjabi is flawless, especially words that I was not supposed to understand, as I might have disapproved. Over time, I became the keeper of secrets, best friend and was no longer considered to be strange. I remember lazy afternoons eating in the neighbours' gardens and laughing at the children spraying water at their cousins. I remember feeling full and sick after weddings that lasted four days and the relentless force to eat during the rounds of Eid visits. Before I left, I thought my roots here to be sturdy and thick. But I learned that older ties to the sea could not be broken and that I needed to have a beach outside of my window.

And strangely, unexpectedly, when you and I made this journey, when I took you to show you this part of my path, you were accepted, embraced as part of me and of course you were fed and quizzed. You were strangely at home with everyone up here and moved with ease amongst the memories of my failures.

Meanwhile, Rosa and I had lost touch. The years drew gentle, imperceptible lines between us, created from distance and time, until neither of us knew where the other one was or what we were doing. Our children grew up and we grew older. But still, we had friends in common and so the news reached me a few days ago. The news that Rosa somehow had died and that today would be the day of her funeral. During my drive on roads that are etched into my memory; on the way that I can take without thinking, I remember Rosa and I remember our journey two winters ago. Of course you were drunk and slept in the car, but you never let go of my hand. I remember pointing to the ice-rink, where Sunday after Sunday my daughters skated for hours so that I could write essays and dissertations. My feet were numb from the cold, but my fingers formed words and arguments about social panic and correlations between wealth and education, class and life expectancy. My daughters became accomplished skaters, whilst I pressed my views on injustice and humanity into quotes.

We follow Rosa's coffin into the light filled room, dominated by a glass wall with views over the lake. Hers embraces her body with woven wicker, laden with wildflowers, seemingly unarranged. Lee, our mutual friend from that time long past, holds me as my face drowns in a torrent of tears. Not just for Rosa, but for you, for us and the beauty of this moment. The moment you should have had, we had planned, envisaged. Not the stiff, violated flowers resting on stark, cold wood with hideous handles. A picture of Rosa, transposed onto the wall shows her smile, the big grin full of life. She has married again, and her three daughters have grown into beautiful, dignified women full of Rosa's grace. The last time, I saw the youngest, she had been in nappies and just learned to make her way on her knees, bumping into the chairs in my kitchen.

There is no reason for them to recognise me, to even remember and I try escape quietly to sit at the side of the lake for a while and conquer the envy that rises in me on our behalf. Lee, however, takes my arm and introduces me to Rosa's husband, who, like me, has to get used to a new title. No longer wife, husband, spouse, partner, but widow, widower, left behind without definition. Suddenly, I find myself embraced and learn that Rosa remembered, her girls remembered – the Christmases, planting daffodils and chasing sunsets and rainbows, the stories told whilst cooking, my strange conversations with Rosa's visiting parents. We did not share any languages but managed to talk for hours about different landscapes and traditions. Rosa's husband tells of memories shared with him and the smiles they brought. The girls recognise me despite the eternity that has passed and I feel that my desire to flee is somehow unfair and selfish. But I flee anyway. I will send them the poems I write about this day, forming them in my head whilst driving back to our cave. I race back to the sea, to you, without stopping to see those I miss as well, those from my other life. I will visit them soon, but for now, I have to run back to the safety of the waves and the wind; must exchange red kites for seagulls.

Travelling with your Ashes

Sheri and I have found a ship in the middle of dense woods. Or at least the stark shape of a ship. Abandoned red bricks, covered in moss and graffiti. Ferns grow from cracks in the stones and missing mortar; windows now hollow eyes in the facade, bereft of wood and glass. The remains of a fireplace, stone and covered and ivy and ferns, give a faint idea to the layout of the building, which once was a church, doubling as a school room during the week. The air should be echoing with the sound of children and a minister, but without a roof, sounds just fly into the canopy of trees, leaving a faint green glow across the soil.

Abandoned, left building a little way away from a village that in itself has no defined outline and seems to float amongst the trees and the sunny valley. No sign of destruction, fire or any other catastrophic event, just left, stripped of wood and glass, or purpose and sense. We sit for a while and ponder over what might have happened, but might have persuaded the villagers to strip the building and then just leave it to nature. It must once have been an important landmark in the life of those who lived around it. It must have seen deaths, baptisms, weddings, budding love and children struggling to learn spellings and licking their tongues whilst playing with numbers. Are walls all we leave behind? I remember visiting a place where the walls had absorbed evil at such a scale that I had to flee. During a cruise on the Main, which I took rather unwillingly, to accompany Jon's mother, the cacti grower, who did not want to travel on her own anymore. We visited charming little villages, impressive castles and the stadium in Nuremburg, the stage of rousing speeches, that changed the world and brought dark clouds over all of humanity. The air itself was dark, the walls still breathing darkness and evil. Like in this beautiful, haunted place, there was no wood, no real indication how the space was used and divided, and yet, it was impossible for me to remain in the confines of the darkened walls. Even if we had not known anything about the events that followed, even if we would have been new and innocent in this world, these walls would have made us shudder. Walls remember, are somehow imprinted with the intentions and thoughts of those, who find shelter amongst them.

The remains of this building are stoic and unconcerned witnesses of human existence, sheltered and hidden as they are amongst the trees and the decaying wood. Somehow time has lost meaning and the ship in the woods remains, not waiting neither for restoration, nor destruction. Sheri and I wonder around the building to find a place for you, where you can rest comfortably and become part of this eternal place that has no grandeur or adoring visitors. We find a small, but deep hollow in one of the trees leaning away from the walls and we release you into the comforting, never ending circle of beginning and end, construction and abandonment. As I climb back towards the car, a small shard of sunshine breaks through the leaves and warms your tree with green light. Here, my Darling, you are as safe as is possible, untouched by human hands and intentions, and I will return to sit next to your tree and maybe read you a story of fairies and butterflies.

And so, my Darling, my Emperor, we stumble through this world, searching for beauty and views, for doors and trees, holy places and different oceans. Whilst I can hope that you somehow have flown into light and peace, I have descended further and further in the dark. Time has not done what they promised me it would do; it has not healed me, but kept the wounds open and weeping. Time has not made the pain ease, just changed it into the numbness of one who should not wander amongst the living anymore. It has made your face fade, but the feeling of your skin under my hands more vivid, more painfully missed.

I have taken their pills, tried to talk to professional listeners, hid in corners and submerged myself in frantic activity. During this spring, I made a garden and hoped you would see it, but apart from a butterfly resting on the spot where your head once lay on the deckchair, nobody has visited. Our hidden garden, full of bees and butterflies, where my hands turn the soil and find nothing. I searched for treasures in flea markets and car boots, finding things you would buy and that now make no sense at all.

I have learned much, searched more, debated and cried, shouted, made myself invisible and laughed at the way you or the universe made some of our adventures impossible. I have learned that kindness is the hardest thing to take when I am vulnerable and weak. Those, who just handed me tissues and held my shoulders grew closer to me than those who tried to make me survive.

Trying to see the world through your eyes, travelling for you, I have realised, that I am not you, these are not your eyes and you might not have enjoyed some of our destinations quite as much as I would have liked you to. But then, you had nothing to compare our journeys to; had only your dreams and our plans. I know you would have loved the wildness of some places and detested the self-importance of others. You have forgiven me for the churches and mosques as we did not visit to pray but to find answers. And I am sure that you would have marvelled over the snow in Bulgaria and laughed at the hours I accidentally spent in a fashion salon in Albania, covered in sequins and glitter, with no way of escape; trapped in a foreign film that politeness stopped me from leaving.

I bought a map and marked the spaces that you inhabit; colourful, small flags covering countries and continents. I have shamelessly used my connections and they allowed me to add a little of you to the bonfire pile that celebrates the harvest and dispels the dangers of the coming winter. A significant event in this seaside town, a tradition, that from now on will secretly also celebrate you amongst the towering flames.

I have let you fly in balloons on New Years Eve, only to find that you were caught in the wind, taking you back inland, with Harry and Emily chasing after your silvery vessels to return you to me and the sea.

We visited the sacred place, where the last dragon was slain and a farmer raced the devil. You are resting in a bench in the shape of the dragon, behind one of his ears, and a little further down a stony path in a lake where the air is full of dragonflies and a Heron watches over your sleep.

And on one of our visits to my former home, north from the beach and our cave, we were blessed to spend some time on a barge, floating silently along the Grand Canal. Suddenly, we moved in a Turner painting of the countryside, with weeping trees and a perfect sky reflected in the clear water. The peace, all-encompassing and eternal, soaked slowly into my skin and my hands did not shake when I left you in this perfect illusion of a world that you never had the chance to explore. On that day, I visited the church next to the tall, forbidding church where my son married many years ago. So much hope for him and his future and the last day that the father of my daughters pretended to stand next to us. The sad cheerfulness of that day still lingers in me as I sit for a while between the bridge over the Thames and the gothic monstrosity of the church. All my children together on that day, accepting my embrace and celebrating hope, none of us aware what was to come and how the wind would take hem away from me, as it has taken you. Only, you and I are travelling together, finding ways to make you matter, and my children grow into their own lives and will have to brace their own pain and gladness, in the measures it is given to them.

And there came a day, when I realised that I would not be able to fill the whole map with you; that this task was just too big for a wounded crow with limited time and even more limited means. Whilst I stared at the globe and wondered about practicalities and destinations, trying to focus on the most important, those who loved you and those who walk beside me became part of our journey. Slowly, imperceptible, others started to help me to make you matter, make the world yours, make you an eternal part of everything and everywhere.

I have to imagine these parts of your travels, but I do have pictures of the places I might never be able to reach, and if my travels should ever take me there, you are already in place, waiting for me. I can imagine your journey to Israel, taken by a friend's parents, who have met neither you nor me. Having read of the thoroughness of Israel's customs and border guards, I had serious misgivings about this particular destination. And yet, you made it and have found a place on the mount of olives, the site of an ascension, you did not believe in. I can picture you, staring wistfully at the graves of the kings of Judah, whilst reflecting on Christ's footprints imprinted on the grey soil and pondering over the Jewish belief that the resurrection of the dead with begin here. How wonderful then that you are here, smiling and being ahead of the living in your knowledge of the truth; whilst I am still clambering amongst the stories and beliefs to find comfort.

And I am envious of your ascent to the ancient monastery in Petra, overlooking the old capital of nomadic people tamed by Romans and Greeks. I would give anything to share the view over the pink stones with you, share a space in one of the caves with your ashes. You travelled through two dangerous borders, nestled against Hannah's toothbrush, into Israel and from there into Jordan. This was a place, you and I mapped out at the top of our explorations and I might never reach. But, I am glad that you are there, in the desert heat, amongst the ancient stones, maybe even watching falcons and at quiet times without tourists, wandering amongst the ghosts of a people long gone.

You reached the Mexican oceans and the coast of Costa Rica, and swim between somewhere between Gibraltar and Morocco. In the pictures Sara and Chloe sent, you join the ocean at sunset, bright oranges and pinks reflecting on the water and I can see us, with our feet in the fine, hot sand, willing the sun to hesitate a while longer and play with the colours and the waves until we tire of the eternal beauty and can sleep under the endless sky. And maybe, one day I can take you myself into the Andes, to the temples hidden under the green of the forests that keep the earth breathing.

You swim with dolphins in the waters of Santini, where Aly took a boat as far as it would go and released you to join a group of your favourite animals. Her voice breaking as she wished you a peaceful journey into the depths of the ocean, and me wishing that you might find Atlantis. During our pandemic months of map reading and ancient texts, we decided that this area might be one of the possible places for this legend to hide from our eyes, visited only by dolphins and shimmering fish.

You travel on the inside of a First Nation drum, snuggly hidden under the hide, you attend powwows with Craig. I sent a wish with you, whispered into some tobacco. A wish for a peaceful journey to wherever you have gone or are still going. Wishing that you will remember my love and the time we had. We so often talked about these nomadic, old cultures and had more than once decided that ultimately, we had to speak to those, who hold oral history that has been passed on from generation to generation. I suspect that there is more truth in any of those narratives than in any of the written accounts of the past, which have been coloured by the intentions and beliefs for the writers and translators. Not many were able to write or to read in the ancient world, and all we know today has been reported through the eyes of those who were privileged. We often talked about Native Americans, Aborigines and other First Nation People, and wanted nothing more than to travel with them for a while; learn their stories about life and death, the beginning of the world and Gods that live in trees and stones. And now you are part of the drumming heartbeat of the travelling story and I am glad.

I wish I had been there when you made your way into the Papal Gardens in Rome. Surely the irony of your presence would not be lost even on the Vatican. You, the ultimate non-believer, the sceptic and critic of all things religious now nestle hidden amongst the flowers, listening to the tinkling of water-features and commenting under your breath on ostentatious beauty and a church that would like to condemn you to eternal darkness. Unmerciful saints, happier to watch people like you in their pain than holding their hand and breathing hope into the lost souls of the lost and the addicts. I am sure, Christ would have embraced you, and maybe still has, whilst those, who claim to speak for him, turn their eyes away and sit in judgement from their splendid gardens and balconies. Ian, who never met you, but would have shared your humour left you in the manicured gardens, where I will not visit you. A joker hidden amongst the bishops, laughing at their theories of afterlife, purgatory and hell.

Harry took you to Tunesia, hot and arid; I am sure you loved the heat and the fact that you now swim unseen and untroubled in the Mediterranean Sea.

You took your life's journey in reverse, when you arrived in Kingston, the town of your parents. Unborn, a small, embryotic promise of life, you left Jamaica in 1958 and returned in a small bottle of grains in 2023. I wonder what you would make of the place of your people, the island you never visited, never wanted to visit. The country, the different world, where you still have living siblings, whom you never met; the city of your mother's past, the beginning of your pain inflicted by those whose dreams brought them to this cold country. I am glad that they did, I am glad for every second we had because in some alternative story, they might not have made their journey and your feet would never have looked for mine during cold winter nights. And as fate unfolds its intricate wings, young Alex was meant to take this journey in the year of the pandemic, whilst we formed Us in the cottage by the sea. In the same way, in which the alternative paths might not have brought you to me, the delay of two years allows you to travel back to your ancestral home.

You spent a day in Mick's trouser pockets, safely tucked away in the dark folds of fabric, whilst I fled from the venue, unable to supress the memory of our wedding. Mick, our witness to promises of lifetimes and travels, married himself on that day, with you in his pockets as his best man. And I know that, next to his happiness, his fingers looked for the small bottle and found you, wishing him luck and happiness.

And you spread your wings on the highest point of Cyprus, where the veterans go, taken by others, in honour and with respect. Flying in the winds, mingling with others who have paid with bad dreams and empty eyes. Shane, fellow searcher for meaning and anchors on the wild waves of warfare and survival, scrambled up the rocky point and allowed you to become part of the rugged landscape, as unsettled and eternal as you.

My sister has taken you to Wisconsin, to the mysteries of forests that are more blue than green, trees, larger than those we knew and a lake the size of an ocean. After many years of little contact, due to the vast distance between Europe and America as well as the different paths we chose, we had two days together, walking, sitting on the beach and learning about the stories of lives lived with our respective nightmares. My sister has chosen a straight path, becoming the glue of her family; my journey, winding and lonely, colourful and confusing has left me with nothing but your ashes. Her husband and her sons hunt and fish and they all like hiking together and I do hope that there is some kind of peace in her future. I am certainly glad that she has taken you to a part of the world, I am very unlikely visit.

I am not sure how you felt about the snow in Bulgaria. Ian took you skiing in the mountains and left you at the top of a slope to watch the falling and melting of snow and ice. You never really liked the cold and found my love for the white stuff amusing, watching me from windows, waiting in the warmth with a coffee and a blanket for me.

Leona our colourful, vulnerable, beautiful friend, who walked beside me for many small parts of my journey, has taken you to Bermuda. You shared the same sense of prickly humour, observed the world through sarcastic, loving eyes and she left you in the botanical gardens. Apparently, you were badly behaved on your journey with her and that does not surprise me in the least. And maybe you might discover the secret of all those disappearing things in the famous triangle in the sun.

Naomi took you to France, where on a grim, grey day, a sunbeam found its way through the clouds and the leaves to warm the spot where she left you. The picture of that moment made me believe that you might, maybe, follow our travels.

I left you in Bremen, not far from my Hometown. A journey with a stranger, who became a friend, to visit my best friend in a hospital. A difficult journey, my head spinning and story to complex and long for even me to understand. I left you near the windmill in the middle of the town, surrounded by tulips and wheeping willows. A town I once knew well, and that has now become bewildering and strange, but, my Darling, I will return, as it is home to two people from different worlds, who are important to me and who were meant to be part of our future. You and I, we were hoping to join them in this nondescript city and build another life.

And of course, you sit with me in the car, always dreaming of one day just simply not coming back to anywhere, staying on the road, finding a place, where we can just be Us. Your travels without me will continue, as well as my travels with you. There is nothing else for me to do, no other purpose, nothing else that might make sense of me and this body that will just not give in.

And so my Darling, my confused, scared hero, I am back in our cave, refusing to turn on the light, just staring at your candle. The small, flickering light that is supposed to guide you back to me. On the outside, my Emperor, my skin is warm and sometimes I laugh. The pain comes in waves, sometimes I feel simply indifferent to everything around me, sometimes I double up, swept away by waves of tears, larger than oceans. I have done my best to make you matter, to tell your story, to make your pain count. And, my Darling, we travel. Maybe one day, I will start travelling just for me again. Maybe one day, I will move your shoes and your clothes. Maybe one day, I might sleep on your side of the bed. But for now, all I have is the hope that you are somewhere where you can play with the stars and might throw one in my direction so that I can know where you are. Just don't send me any more feathers, I cannot tell the difference between those that just fell off birds and those you might have send for me to find. I will look after your mother's grave, however much I dislike my journeys to Croydon. And maybe I find the strength of see our consultant to explain the pictures to me that showed him what was growing in you, because I need to know if there would have been anything I could have done, apart from stroking your arm and watch your pulse stop at 19:54.

ACKNOWLEDGMENTS

There are really too many kind souls to mention and even beginning to do so would do so many others injustice. But, I am grateful for every coffee, every warm embrace, every book some of you sent, every text message and all of the time you have spent with me, talking about Everton. Talking about him, being allowed to do so without embarrassment and to learn irreverence has kept me going.

And of course, without Buster, Snowy and Hannibal, allowing me to cry into their fleeces, I would not have been able to make it this far.

Some people have travelled with me, some for me and some have just been there. You will find yourself in these pages and I will forever love you for the support that I deserved so little and sometimes rejected. My students, my dear friends Carly and Javene have kept me on my toes; Wendy has allowed me to cry all over her beautiful kitchen; Sarah, whom I have never met, sent a beautiful book and checked in on me. Stephen, my wonderful best friend, thank you for sending me daily emoji flowers, just to remind me that you are there.

ABOUT THE AUTHOR

Heike Rentel grew up partly in Hamburg and partly in the countryside of the most northern parts of Germany. She currently lives on the South Coast of the UK, teaching, writing and collecting feathers.

Printed in Great Britain
by Amazon